*Oral Presentations in the
Composition Course*
A BRIEF GUIDE

Oral Presentations in the Composition Course

A BRIEF GUIDE

Matthew Duncan
Northern Illinois University

Gustav W. Friedrich
Rutgers University

Bedford/St. Martin's   Boston ◆ New York

For Bedford/St. Martin's

Developmental Editor: Caroline Thompson
Production Editor: Kerri A. Cardone
Senior Production Supervisor: Joe Ford
Marketing Manager: Kevin Feyen
Editorial Assistant: Jennifer Lyford
Copyeditor: Lisa Wehrle
Text Design and Compostion: Claire Seng-Niemoeller
Cover Design: Donna Dennison, Kim Cevoli
Printing and Binding: Malloy Lithographing

President: Joan E. Feinberg
Editorial Director: Denise B. Wydra
Editor in Chief: Karen S. Henry
Director of Marketing: Karen Melton Soeltz
Director of Editing, Design, and Production: Marcia Cohen
Managing Editor: Elizabeth M. Schaaf

Library of Congress Control Number: 2005938006

Manufactured in the United States of America.

6 5

m

For information, write: Bedford/St. Martin's, 75 Arlington Street,
Boston, MA 02116   (617-399-4000)

ISBN-10:   0-312-41784-5
ISBN-13:   978-0-312-41784-0

Contents

Introduction   1

1. Choosing a Topic   3

Brainstorming   3
Consulting with Others   4
Researching Ideas   4
Making a Choice   5

2. Determining Your Purpose   6

Informative Presentations   8
   Description   8
   Demonstration   10
   Definition   11
   Explanation   13
Persuasive Presentations   14
   Propositions of Fact   14
   Propositions of Value   14
   Concerns about a Problem   15
   Propositions of Policy   15
A Final Word   16

3. Analyzing Your Audience   17

Types of Audiences   18
   The Selected Audience and the Concerted Audience   18
   The Passive Audience   19
   The Pedestrian Audience and the Organized Audience   19

◆ BOX: Audience Characteristics and Strategies   20

Audience Attitudes   21

Hostile Audiences   22

Sympathetic Audiences   22

Neutral Audiences   23

Communication Barriers   23

Barriers That Involve Content   24

Barriers That Involve Audience and Delivery   27

4. Adapting Your Ideas and Evidence   29

Listening and Learning   29

Choosing Forms of Support   30

Explanation   30

Examples   31

Statistics   32

Testimony   35

Visual Aids   36

Choosing Forms of Proof   36

Motivational Proof or Pathos   37

Ethical Proof or Ethos   37

Logical Proof or Logos   38

5. Organizing Your Presentation   40

Creating an Outline   40

Choosing an Organizational Pattern   43

Chronological Pattern   44

Topical Pattern   44

Spatial or Geographical Pattern   45

Cause-Effect Pattern   45

Problem-Solution Pattern   45

Compare and Contrast Pattern   46

◆ BOX: Patterns of Organization   46

6. Developing Effective Introductions, Transitions, and Conclusions   49

The Introduction   49
Language Choices   52
Transitions   54
The Conclusion   55

7. Using Visual Aids   57

Choosing Effective Visuals   57
Choosing a Mode of Delivery   59
  Chalkboard or Whiteboard   59
  Handouts   59
  Overhead Transparencies   60
  Presentation Software   61
Designing Visual Aids   64
  Fonts   64
  Contrast and Spacing   65
  Color   65
  Images   66
Avoiding Technical Problems   66

8. Practicing, Polishing, and Delivering the Presentation   68

Modes of Speaking   68
  Impromptu Speaking   68
  Extemporaneous Speaking   70
  Scripted Speaking   71
  Memorized Speaking   72
Voice and Body Language   73
Dealing with Stage Fright   74
Polishing the Presentation   76

9. Presenting as a Group 78

Dividing the Work 78
Transitioning between Speakers 80
Acknowledging Nonspeaking Group Members 81

10. Evaluating Presentations 82

Checklist for Evaluating a Presentation 83
  The Speaker's Delivery 83
  Content and Coherence 84
  Argument and Persuasion 85
Thinking Critically about Your Own Presentation 86

Introduction

In your composition course, you are asked to write a number of different types of papers for different purposes. Your assignments probably include personal essays, descriptions, arguments, research papers, literary papers, or multimedia projects. Many of these and other modes of writing lend themselves to oral presentations such as leading a class discussion after researching a topic, talking about a paper in progress, or presenting a final writing project. You already may have taken a public speaking course, or perhaps you will take such a course later. Outside of your college courses, you are also likely to be asked to speak in front of a group. One of the most practical applications of a composition course is authoring and developing speeches and presentations. Many professions and disciplines require presentations, from sales to human resources training, from advertising to politics, from psychology to biology. Both modes of communication—writing and speaking—are critically important no matter where your plans after college take you, and neither happens in isolation.

This supplement offers guidelines and strategies for adapting your written research, analyses, and arguments for oral presentations. You will recognize some of this information since many of the strategies for creating good oral presentations are the same as those for writing good compositions. Even if you have not already written a paper about your topic, this guide will help you develop a presentation from brainstorming through organization to delivery.

This supplement prepares you to do the following:

- Identify a specific purpose and topic for an oral presentation and select an organizational pattern

- Analyze audiences in terms of their expectations, attitudes toward your position, and group cohesiveness

- Construct and adapt outlines for oral presentations

- Compose effective introductions, transitions, and conclusions

- Incorporate effective visual aids into your presentation

- Describe four modes of speaking and how they are effective for different situations

- Understand how your voice and body language affect your audience

- Cope with nervousness and stage fright

- Organize an effective group presentation

- Evaluate presentations made by your fellow students and other speakers

Choosing a Topic 1

The first step in preparing any oral presentation is to carefully read the assignment. What is it asking you to do? Inform your audience about a topic? Persuade them to change their thinking about an issue? If you are unsure about any of the assignment's requirements, ask your instructor for clarification (and do so well in advance of the due date!). Remember, too, that the requirements for your written composition assignment may differ from those for your oral presentation. Only after you understand what the assignment is asking you to do can you narrow your focus to find a good topic.

And what's a good topic? One that fulfills the requirements of your assignment, one that is manageable and specific, and one that you know something about and are interested in. You'll notice that these are the same qualities you use when choosing a topic for an essay or research paper.

In searching for a good topic, try the following strategies for generating ideas: brainstorming, consulting with others, and researching ideas.

Brainstorming

Brainstorming—listing any topic ideas that occur to you, without censoring yourself—starts by examining your own interests and expertise. What are you interested in? What would you like to find out more about? What are your experiences? What do you know? (Be sure to distinguish between what you know and what you believe: Knowledge is based on facts that you can support; belief is based on values and opinions.) In addition to listing your ideas, you could try grouping them in clusters and mapping their connections to one another. These visual types of brainstorming strategies may reveal emergent connections you hadn't originally considered.

For example, assume that the assignment requires you to give a 2- to 3-minute speech describing a place. In choosing a topic, begin to think about this assignment from your personal experiences. What places do you know around your college or university? Your local community? Your state? The United States? Other countries? Also ask yourself what places, in each of these settings, you would like to know more about.

As you brainstorm, avoid evaluation and judgment (for example, "The class won't want to know about that!" or "The teacher already knows this!"). Just write down as many ideas as you can. Evaluation comes later, when you sort through the multiple possibilities to find the one topic that will become your focus.

Consulting with Others

Conversations with friends, classmates, professors, family members, and others can be important sources of topics for oral presentations. Not only can consulting with others help you generate topics that you may not think of on your own, but also, by providing your first "audience," it can help you evaluate the potential value of topics.

Researching Ideas

Another valuable source of topics for presentations is the library's collection of books, journals, online databases, and other materials. Sometimes just browsing through current newspapers and periodicals will remind you of or spark your interest in a particular topic. The reference librarian can also advise you on library resources. The Internet, especially the World Wide Web, may also help you explore ideas for your presentation. But do not rely too heavily on the Web for inspiration. Although a huge amount of free information is available online almost immediately, much of the Web lacks the editorial standards and fact-checking requirements of traditional print media. If you find good ideas through a Web search, be sure to follow up on those ideas at the library.

Making a Choice

You have searched for potential topics by solo brainstorming, talking with others, searching online, and visiting the library. The next task is crucial and perhaps the most difficult of all. You must filter all the information you have gathered and select the topic that best meets the following three criteria:

1. Is it a topic you are interested in and know something about?
2. Is it a topic that satisfies the requirements specified in the assignment?
3. Is it a topic that your audience will find worthwhile?

Once you have chosen an appropriate topic, you will need to narrow your focus to begin developing your thesis for your paper (if the assignment calls for one) or your presentation. Writing guides and handbooks are good sources of information for advice on developing an effective thesis or presentation.

2 Determining Your Purpose

If your oral presentation is based on a paper you've written for your composition course, you may feel that the best course is merely to read the paper to the class. Few things, however, are more tedious and less engaging than listening to someone read a research paper aloud. Multiply that by the number of students in your class and you can understand why oral presentations take more preparation and consideration.

When you give your oral presentation, you must articulate the main idea of your paper in a statement of specific purpose—a single declarative sentence that specifies what you expect the audience to know, do, believe, and feel after you speak. Here are some examples:

- "I want the audience to know about the history and current use of inline skates."

- "I want the audience to vote against repealing Title IX."

- "I want the audience to understand the various meanings of the word *communication*."

- "I want the audience to understand what AIDS is and what we need to do to prevent it from spreading."

- "I want the audience to appreciate the contributions of Eleanor Roosevelt to our society."

Your paper should have a thesis statement—a sentence that summarizes what you want the audience to get out of your oral presentation. Whereas the specific purpose summarizes how you want your audience to respond to your oral presentation (for example, "I want the audience to vote for Joyce Jones for Congress"), your thesis statement captures what you want your audience to remember even if they later forgot much of the rest of what you said ("I want the audience to vote for Joyce Jones for Congress *because* she is honest, informed, and effective"). If you do not already have a clear, concise thesis statement in your paper, consider revising your introduction. When you are giving the presentation, stick to your thesis statement. Make it obvious to your audience that this is your purpose and goal.

Presentations usually have one of two general purposes: to inform or to persuade. Oral presentations that inform try to provide audiences with information that they will find new, relevant, and useful. Such presentations can take a variety of forms. For example, a presentation could explain a process, such as how to play various styles of music on the guitar, how to change the oil in a car, or how to mix music and scratch using two turntables. It could describe objects or places, like the Vietnam Memorial, inline skates, or the beach in Cancun. Informative presentations often define things, for example, hip hop, coordinating conjunctions, or the field of communication studies. Informative presentations also attempt to answer questions that we have about the world: What are tidal waves? What was the impact of Martin Luther King Jr.'s "I Have a Dream" speech? What are the differences between computer hacking and cracking?

While informative presentations deal with facts and procedures, persuasive writing and speaking focus on beliefs, values, and opinions. Instead of describing what exists, persuasion focuses on building a case for what should be. Although persuasive presentations most frequently ask for a change in belief, attitude, or behavior ("Boycott this corporation to protest its monopolistic practices"), they can also reaffirm existing attitudes and actions ("We should continue to use the existing grading structure at our university").

Informative Presentations

Informative presentations generally take one of four forms: description, demonstration, definition, or explanation. As you read the following discussions of these forms, keep in mind that you may need to combine them depending on the topic of your informative presentation.

Description

Description is one of the most basic categories for presenting information. Description requires you to put into words what you have experienced with your senses. You want your audience to feel, hear, and see what you felt, heard, and saw. You must have a clear idea of what you want to describe and why, and you should emphasize vital details and eliminate the trivial ones. In choosing which details to use, carefully consider your audience. Details that one audience finds clear and vivid another may find less so. (See Chapter 3 for more on analyzing your audience.)

Following is an excerpt from a descriptive speech by Major James N. Rowe; it was delivered to students of the U.S. Army General Staff and Command College at Leavenworth, Kansas. Major Rowe delivered the speech extemporaneously—that is, he prepared his ideas in advance but composed his precise wording at the moment he spoke. Notice how he calls up details of his surroundings and his feelings as he describes his experience as a U.S. prisoner of war in South Vietnam.

> Now, in the camp, the physical conditions in South Vietnam with the Viet Cong are primitive. I was in the U Minh Forest; the camps were temporary at best. You had two to three feet of standing water during the rainy season; in the dry season it sank out, and you were hunting for drinking water. We had two meals of rice a day, and generally we got salt and nuoc mam [a fish sauce used to flavor food] with them. We did get infrequent fish from the guards, but always the castoff that the guards didn't want. If we got greens, it was maybe one meal's worth every two or three months. Immediately vitamin deficiency and malnutri-

tion were a problem. This is a thing you are going to fight the whole way through. And you are fighting on two sides. You are fighting for physical survival, and you are fighting for mental survival. The physical survival is just staying alive. We found that we had to eat a quart pan of rice each meal, two meals a day, just to stay alive. We found that [we did better] if we could put down everything we had, and I think the most difficult thing initially was the nuoc mam. It is high in protein value, but the VC don't have that much money to spend on nuoc mam. You don't get Saigon nuoc mam. Theirs is called ten-meter nuoc mam. You can smell it within ten meters, and it is either repulsive or inedible, depending on how long you have been there. But this was the type of thing you are eating for nutritional value, and not for taste. So you are fighting on that side.[1]

Note Major Rowe's choice of words at the outset, "the physical conditions . . . are primitive." The rest of this passage fleshes out this statement. Rowe describes first the environmental conditions of rising and falling water levels. He bases his definition of "primitive" on two basic human needs, shelter and food. The majority of the passage deals with food, a choice that offers his audience compelling examples to which they can relate. Rowe moves from the general (a broad overview of the climate) to the very specific (nuoc mam). He even uses wry, dark humor as a subtle example of a survival technique—the prisoners' name for the fish sauce, "ten-meter nuoc mam," is a grim joke about the smell. This final sensory description will linger with a listener and draw the audience in to the rest of Rowe's presentation.

Presentations about literature or film are often descriptive. Poetry analysis is one type of descriptive process that uses a very specific format and vocabulary. By identifying the meter and rhyme scheme in a poem, a writer is describing the poem's technical features. The same is usually true when discussing the lighting, cinematography, or dialogue in a film or television show. Usually, academic writing assignments involve some degree of description along with some other mode, such as definition or explanation.

[1] Richard L. Johannesen, R. R. Allen, and Wil L. Linkugel, *Contemporary American Speeches,* 7th ed. (Dubuque, IA: Kendall/Hunt, 1992) 52.

Demonstration

Demonstration presentations narrate how to do something. Giving a demonstration presentation seems natural and easy enough. After all, if we have figured out how things happen or work, we should be able to explain them to others! If we know how to get to the mall, we should be able to tell another person how to get there. Unfortunately, as you know, this is not always the case.

To prepare a demonstration presentation, start by identifying your audience and their level of knowledge about your topic. For example, if you are giving directions to a location in Chicago, you must first assess the audience's familiarity with Chicago before referring to "The Eisenhower" rather than "I-290." Similarly, if you are working with a computer novice, you probably should use "turn the computer on" instead of "boot the machine." With a clear statement of purpose in mind, give a broad outline of the process and discuss the major steps in chronological order. Use transitional words such as "first . . . , next . . . , finally . . ." (see Chapter 6). Be sure your language is appropriate for your audience; when necessary, define terms. Do not dwell on insignificant details. Relate each major step to the whole process. Occasionally, remind the audience where you are in the process.

The following outline of the first steps in the printmaking process of producing woodcuts illustrates a demonstration speech. You can imagine the speaker showing each step.

A. To prepare the block

   1. Use a power sander to smooth rough, scratched, or dented boards.

   2. Lightly sandpaper the surface to ensure an even flatness.

   3. To enhance the grain quality in prints, run a wire brush over the surface in the direction of the grain.

B. To transfer the design, use one of three methods.

   1. Coat the block with white gouache, and draw directly on it.

    2. Place carbon paper on the block, then your drawing, then tracing paper; press firmly with a pencil to draw in the main elements.

    3. Paste the drawing onto the surface of the block and cut away the white areas.

  C. To cut the block

    1. Hold the knife with your forefinger along the top of the blade to apply downward pressure, and use your other fingers as guides.

    2. Use a gouge by gently tapping it with a mallet; always direct the point of the tool away from your body.[2]

As you might guess, demonstration presentations often rely heavily on the use of visual aids and handouts. (See Chapter 7 for more about using visual aids.) Demonstration presentations also often involve specialized vocabulary. *Gouache* stands out in the example above, but some audiences may not even be familiar with tools like *power sanders, mallets,* and *gouges.* When making a demonstration presentation, define your terms first and repeat their definitions when you use them again. Another good idea when making a demonstration presentation is to move slowly and deliberately through each step of the process. If your audience is attempting to work along with you, pause or ask them whether they need more time before you continue.

Definition

Definition involves answering questions like "What is this thing?" Formal definitions—those found in dictionaries—have three parts: the name of the thing, the class or group to which it belongs, and the qualities that distinguish it from other members of its class. Thus, to define *notation,* you could say that it is "a system of figures or symbols used to represent numbers, quantities, etc."

[2] Adapted from Bruce Robertson and David Gormley, *Step-by-Step Printmaking* (London: Diagram Visual Information Ltd., 1987) 71.

Thing	Class or group	Qualities
Notation is	a system of figures or symbols	used to represent numbers, quantities, etc.

But simple definitions like these are often inadequate for describing complex ideas. Figures of speech—metaphors, similes, analogies, and the like—can help listeners understand complex concepts. You can compare and contrast a term with similar ones or use examples. Because your task is to establish a meaning the audience will understand and accept, you need to be as specific and concrete as possible. Defining an *ollie* as "a skateboard trick" is inadequate; a much better definition includes details about the placement of the skater's feet and the motion of one foot kicking downward to snap the tail of the board against the ground while the other foot slides along the board as it rises off the ground. Even comparing the trick to a short hopping jump makes the image of an ollie clearer to your audience.

Robert M. White, then president of the National Academy of Engineering, defined *invention* in the following excerpt from his speech, "Inventors, Invention, and Innovation":

> Invention is more than the development of useful and productive devices, although these are vital for material progress. Instead, it is a manifestation of the creativity in all human activities. The invention of the Gothic arch permitted the soaring cathedrals of the Middle Ages and the Renaissance. The paintings of Monet and Pissarro brought us the glories of impressionism. Our daily lives are uplifted by the songs of Irving Berlin and the symphonies of Beethoven.
>
> In short, invention is where you find it. And so it is in industry. Whatever the function, whether in research and development, design, production, or distribution of goods and services, inventions are at the root of new products and processes and also the source of the economic success of companies. Inventions are the lifeblood coursing through the heart of industrial competitiveness.[3]

[3] Johannesen, Allen, and Linkugel 66.

Note that White begins with a practical definition of invention, "the development of useful and productive devices." He qualifies that definition by adding the complex abstract idea "manifestation of creativity." By using the examples of the Gothic arch and Monet paintings, he illustrates—makes concrete—his complex idea. White goes on to summarize his definition by applying it, making it real for his audience and offering good reasons why they should care about invention.

Explanation

An explanatory presentation may seem similar to a descriptive presentation, but describing how to surf the Web, for example, is fundamentally different from explaining how Web browsers interpret HTML to display Web sites. Describing how to surf the Web creates awareness. Explaining how it works creates understanding. Explanatory speeches create understanding in an audience because they answer the questions "Why?" or "What does that mean?" They typically deal with problems and with plans and policies. Thus, they are usually more abstract than descriptive and demonstration speeches. The challenge to the speaker is to explain a problem, action, or decision without persuading the audience.

There are at least three ways in which answers to "why" questions may be difficult for uninitiated audiences to understand:

1. They may have difficulty in understanding the meaning and use of a term.
2. They may have difficulty abstracting the main points from complex information.
3. They may be hesitant to accept an implausible proposition (such as Einstein's notion that we are accelerating toward the center of the earth).

Your challenge as an explanatory speaker is to assess the main difficulty facing the audience and to shape the presentation to overcome that difficulty.

Persuasive Presentations

As we know from the discussion of informative oral presentations, the task of an informative speaker is to present information in such a fashion that an audience will focus on, understand, and remember it. The persuasive speaker has a different task: to present a message that, if accepted, requires the audience to change beliefs, attitudes, values, or behaviors. Historically, persuasive messages have been categorized according to four types: propositions of fact, propositions of value, concerns about a problem, and propositions of policy.[4]

Propositions of Fact

Propositions of fact make and support claims. That is, you pose and answer the questions "Was it true? Is it true? and Will it be true?" The supposed fact that you want the audience to accept as true can concern an individual, an event, a process, a condition, a concept, or a policy. The following are examples of propositions that claim the existence of a fact:

- "The federal government has evidence that flying saucers are real."

- "Workers in smoky bars and restaurants face a great risk of lung cancer."

- "Your dealership will lose money on its sales of compact cars because your inventory is too small."

Propositions of Value

Propositions of value make evaluative assertions. That is, they answer the questions "How important is it?" and "What is its worth?" In presentations of this type, you seek to convince an audience of something's specific degree of goodness or quality: an individual, an event, an object, a way of life, a process, a condition, or

[4] Johannesen, Allen, and Linkugel.

another value. You can urge your audience to adopt a new value or, through redefining an old value, to change their perspective. You can also motivate your audience to renew their commitment to a value they already hold. Consider the following examples:

- "Lee Jones is the best professor in our English department."

- "Nuclear weapons are immoral."

- "Organized religion has produced more harm than good."

Concerns about a Problem

Presentations that create concern about a problem usually define a situation and add more information to raise awareness. They answer the question "What is it?" Such presentations ask an audience to agree that specific conditions should be perceived as a problem requiring a solution. In addition to making a compelling presentation concerning the nature of the problem, such presentations attempt to create concern by showing the impact of the problem on the audience. The following are examples of propositions asserting problems:

- "The United States' sale of arms to other countries is a cause for concern."

- "Sexual harassment is a continuing problem on college and university campuses."

- "We should be concerned about the depiction of violence on children's television shows."

Propositions of Policy

In presentations that affirm propositions of policy, you advocate adoption of a new policy. That is, you answer the question "What course of action should be pursued?" Additionally, you can recommend continuing or discontinuing an existing policy or rejecting a proposed one. Your task as the speaker is to promote a course of action or policy as necessary and desirable (or unnecessary and undesirable). Examples of such propositions include the following:

- "Gays and lesbians should have the same rights as all U.S. citizens."

- "Colleges and universities should not limit free speech."

- "Certain illegal drugs such as marijuana should be legalized for medicinal purposes."

A Final Word

Presentations, like the papers you write in composition class, tend to fall into the two general categories—informative presentations and persuasive presentations—discussed in this chapter. But few of the presentations you make (or papers you write) will fit perfectly within one category, subcategory, or style of presentation. An informative presentation, for example, may raise questions whose answers require a more persuasive approach. Or a presentation about an e. e. cummings sonnet may require several different informative strategies: definition (of *sonnet*), description (of the elements in a sonnet), and explanation (of why cummings's use of the sonnet form is surprising). Likewise, a persuasive presentation may use several informative techniques. Or a topic in one of the four persuasive subcategories may easily fit into another.

No matter which type (or types) of presentation you prepare, make your purpose and goal obvious to your audience. Everything you say during the presentation, all the examples you offer, and all the visual aids or handouts you use should focus on your thesis and purpose. Before you give your presentation, be sure that you can clearly state in your own words the point you are trying to make. Keep this point always in mind as you write your paper, as you adapt the presentation from your paper, and as you deliver the presentation.

Analyzing Your Audience 3

Public speaking audiences base their expectations on many factors, which include internal as well as external ones. Audience members' existing beliefs and values, their knowledge (or lack of knowledge) about the speaker or topic, events happening in the outside world, and even the time of day or comfort of the speaking room all influence an audience's expectations. You need to know about these expectations in order to fulfill or deal with them. For every speaking situation, therefore, it is important to ask these questions:

- Why are members of the audience here?
- What are they expecting to hear in this kind of situation?
- What expectations do they have about me?
- What are they expecting to hear from me on this topic?
- What features of the environment (both internal to the speaking room and external to it) might affect audience expectations?
- In what ways will it benefit my presentation or argument to fulfill the audience's expectations?
- In what ways will it benefit my presentation or argument to violate these expectations? (For example, if your audience expects to be bored by a dry and lifeless presentation, how can you confront their expectations?)

How do you determine the beliefs, attitudes, values, experiences, and needs of an audience? One way to begin is to classify the audience in terms of its cohesiveness or togetherness. You can group audiences into five types: selected, concerted, passive, pedestrian, or organized.[1] Whatever its type, any audience will also have an existing attitude toward your position or topic—hostile, sympathetic, or neutral. In the following sections, we look first at the five types of audiences and then at audience attitudes.

Types of Audiences

The Selected Audience and the Concerted Audience

In a selected audience, the speaker and audience share a common and known purpose, but they do not necessarily agree on the best way to achieve their shared goals. As Democrats or Republicans gather at their convention, for example, they agree, in general, on what will help get their party's candidates elected. Nevertheless, as they work on the party platform, many disagreements arise concerning the best approach to take on issues like the economy or defense policy. Thus, your first task when addressing a selected audience is to channel any shared motives into a direction you have planned and developed.

The concerted audience is a subset of a selected audience and is therefore quite similar to it. Its members share a need to achieve some end and are usually positively disposed toward the speaker and the topic. They are inclined to do what the speaker suggests, but they still need to be convinced. When members of the Republican Party meet to put together a party platform, they are a selected audience—they have a common goal. But different wings of the party are likely to have different concerns about what should be included in the platform—each wing is a concerted audience. Your task when addressing a concerted audience is to capitalize on the audience's predisposition to accept your ideas.

Selected and concerted audiences are not common in a classroom setting, but it may be to your advantage to consider treating your classmates as one of these types of audiences. Ideally, all students at a university or college should share some goals and values.

---

[1] Harry L. Hollingsworth, *The Psychology of the Audience* (New York: American Book, 1935).

In particular, everyone is there to learn and grow. While this may seem idealistic, you should work from this basic assumption that your audience is invested in learning. The more you invest in your topic and your presentation, the more likely it is that your peers will be engaged and respond to your message.

The Passive Audience

In a classroom setting, you are most likely to encounter a passive audience. The passive audience is a group that is already gathered to hear the speaker, but its motivation level is low. When you speak in class, for example, an attendance requirement guarantees you the presence of an audience; it does not guarantee, however, that your audience will be interested in everything (or anything!) you have to say. Any time you address a passive audience, your first goal is to gain their attention. Then, your main task is to sustain and direct listeners' interest.

One way to sustain the interest of a passive audience is to treat them the way you might treat a selected or concerted audience. By speaking as if your audience shares your purpose, you change not only your expectations about the audience, but also their potential responses to your message or argument. Making a presentation to a class is a type of performance. You can shape an audience's response to your message by treating them as if they are already allies (as with a concerted audience). If the demeanor of your presentation positions your audience as sympathetic, but acknowledges a need to allay fears or address concerns (as with a selected audience), even the harshest critics may respond more favorably. But a skilled public speaker never assumes too much about an audience. While this tactic may work more successfully in a first-year composition class, a careful and practiced speaker will treat each presentation separately and analyze each audience carefully.

The Pedestrian Audience and the Organized Audience

The least cohesive group is the pedestrian audience—people who have no obvious connection with either the speaker or one another. For example, a fundamentalist preacher might stand on a busy

Audience Characteristics and Strategies

	Characteristics	Examples	Strategies
Selected	• Speaker and audience share a common and known purpose • Speaker and audience do not necessarily agree on best way to achieve shared goals	• Political party convention attendees • Students attending a campus meeting to discuss a specific problem	• Channel any shared motives into a planned and developed direction • Treat as sympathetic, but acknowledge need to calm fears or address concerns
Concerted	• Subset of a *selected* audience • Members share a need to achieve some end • Usually positively disposed toward the speaker and the topic • Inclined to do what the speaker suggests, but still need to be convinced	• A faction within a political party • A division within a company • Members of a campus club or organization	• Treat as if already allies • Capitalize on expected willingness to accept your ideas
Passive	• Already gathered to hear the speaker • Motivation level is low	• Your classmates • Office staff	• Capture their attention • Sustain and direct interest • Consider treating as *selected* or *concerted* (see above)
Pedestrian	• No obvious connection with either the speaker or one another • Least cohesive group	• Passersby on a street corner • People on the subway	• Work to attract the audience • Entertain them • Invite controversy
Organized	• Completely devoted to the speaker and to the speaker's purpose • Most cohesive group	• Some religious groups • Fan clubs	• Focus less on informing and persuading • Celebrate with them

street corner and attempt to attract a pedestrian audience (literally) by vividly describing people's sins and their need for salvation. Most of us are familiar with how such an audience reacts. At the other end of the spectrum is the organized audience. Organized audiences are completely devoted to the speaker and to the speaker's purpose. Some religious and political groups fall into this category, as do audiences who have committed themselves to a noncontroversial cause, such as honoring basketball star Allen Iverson on his birthday. Thus, informing and persuading organized audiences is typically less important than celebrating with them. An extreme such as the pedestrian or organized audience is unlikely in a classroom situation. Your audience is most likely to be passive, and in ideal situations, the audience may be selected or concerted.

Audience Attitudes

Identifying the type of audience you are facing is an important component of audience analysis, but it is only the first step. You also need to discover your audience's attitude toward and knowledge about your topic:

- A *hostile* audience is resistant to your message.
- A *sympathetic* audience probably already agrees with many of the points you are making, or at least is willing to listen to your position.
- A *neutral* audience does not have strong feelings one way or another.

Not every member of an audience need share the same disposition, but the prevailing attitude of the audience is important to identify and acknowledge. The degree to which your audience is hostile, sympathetic, or neutral to your message can have a dramatic effect on how you deliver it.

The audience's attitude is sometimes difficult to predict, but often depends on the level of controversy surrounding your topic. You may have to assess the audience as you make the presentation and meet their reactions with your own counterresponses. Keep in mind that the audience's attitude toward your message is independent of what type of audience they are. For example, your class may be a passive audience, but they may also be hostile to your message. They just may not care to voice those differing perspectives. A passive audience may also be sympathetic, which may greatly decrease the dynamic feedback they offer. And a pedestrian audience is not always going to be neutral. Usually, any audience is made up of a mixture of hostile, sympathetic, and neutral members. Small clusters of any faction, though, may influence your presentation.

Hostile Audiences

Although hostile audiences are not necessarily angry with the speaker or throwing rotten tomatoes, they do begin the presentation with a bias against the message of the speaker. Hostile audiences often offer feedback with their body language, for example, by looking away from the speaker, sitting with their arms crossed, or scowling and shaking their heads. Facing a hostile audience is challenging, but it also provides a potential source of energy for your presentation. The tension between the audience and your message can invigorate your delivery. A hostile audience is likely to pay more attention to your presentation, if only to scrutinize every detail and pick apart your arguments. Do not let the hostility of the audience members shake your delivery style; do not let any hostile audience members derail your train of thought or lead you off on unrelated tangents. Be prepared to answer a number of questions.

Sympathetic Audiences

Sympathetic audiences agree with at least the main idea of the presentation. Their opinions may still differ from that expressed in your presentation, but they are willing to listen to and consider your message with open minds. The fact that the audience is sympathetic may not be the most beneficial situation, though, for a dynamic or rousing presentation. If the audience is so sympathetic that they already know the details you are presenting or they feel that what you are arguing is a foregone conclusion, then you may find them becoming hostile, not to your message, but to the situation. They may feel that you are "preaching to the choir" and question your choice of subject. They may also become (or remain) passive. If you know in advance that the audience is sympathetic, do not rely on their body language or feedback to drive your delivery. Instead, keep them engaged through interesting new insights, dynamic body language and verbal delivery, and challenging explorations of the merits of the opposing arguments.

Neutral Audiences

Many audiences are neutral to your message. They may have no previous knowledge about your topic or have no firm opinions about the subject matter. The neutral audience is possibly the most interesting group to address because the substance of your presentation is likely to help sway their opinions one way or another. The next time you address this audience about the same subject matter, they may have shifted from neutral to sympathetic. Many of the challenges faced in dealing with a passive audience are also present with a neutral audience. Your main tasks are to gain the neutral audience's attention and to sustain their interest.

Communication Barriers

Communication barriers are problems that prevent you from getting your message across or that prevent your audience from responding in the way you hope. Listed on the next page are eight of the most common communication barriers that speakers encounter.[2] Most of these barriers arise from extremes and are resolved by seeking balance and compromise.

---

[2] R. P. Hart, *Lecturing as Communication,* unpublished manuscript, Purdue University, Purdue Research Foundation, 1975.

Barriers that involve content

- Too much or too little information

- Information is fact-heavy or opinion-heavy

- Information is too concrete or too abstract

- Information is too general or too specific

Barriers that involve audience and delivery

- Level of feedback from the audience

- Pace of presentation

- Chronology and logical organization

- Intensity of speaker's delivery

Barriers That Involve Content

Your choices of information to include in an oral presentation may elicit the following communication barriers.

- *Too much information.* "Information overload" produces frustration as an audience feels buried by an avalanche of information and stops listening. You must analyze, filter, and succinctly and precisely deliver information in order for it to become useful knowledge. Your audience is attempting to analyze and filter that same information based on what you say and how you say it.

    EXPLAIN SPECIALIZED LANGUAGE: Technical jargon and acronyms (mp3, AAC, RIAA, MPAA, 802.11b, IEEE 1394, etc.) are often confusing. Handouts or visual aids are useful for defining terms and abbreviations. (See Chapter 7 for more about using visual aids.)

    AVOID UNNECESSARY DETAILS: When giving a 5-minute presentation on copyright and media licensing, do not spend most of your time citing Senate propositions and House bills by number and date. Instead, give a broad overview with general terms and a handout with links and citations for more information to make your point more effectively.

- *Too little information.* Be aware of your audience's level of expertise and present enough information to challenge the average member. If you do not have enough information, you risk boring or insulting your audience. It is unlikely that you will complete the requirements of the assignment if you have too little information. But be careful not to confuse clarity and precision with having too little information. Seek a balance between "overload" and "skimming the surface."

  DEFINE NEW TERMS: Take time when introducing each new term in context. Again, handouts are useful, as are projected presentations (PowerPoint, overheads, etc.). If the terms are not new for your audience, move more quickly through the material.

  STAY FOCUSED: If your task is to compare and contrast the features of several blog service providers, spend only one paragraph in your paper, and one slide in your software or overhead presentation, defining a blog as a "web log" or online journal. Make the majority of the paper or presentation about the various service providers, not the uses of blogs, especially in a course about online communication.

- *Information is too factual or too inferential.* Ideal speakers are neither fact-spewing computers nor rambling philosophers. Rather, they know how to extend their listeners' knowledge by blending hard data and intelligent speculation. Most audiences want enough facts to support your inferences and enough inferences to answer the question "So what?" about the facts.

  MAKE FACTS EASY TO DIGEST: Consider placing numerical or statistical facts in a chart or graph. Audiences respond better to visualized information, especially when confronted with many numbers and figures.

  USE SOUND LOGIC: Do not fall into the trap of logical fallacies. Does your data really support what you are saying, or is it just conveniently similar to your own opinion? (For more about providing logical evidence, see Chapter 4.)

- *Information is too concrete or too abstract.* Curious, searching audiences demand that speakers satisfy their needs for both concrete and abstract information. If you carefully mix and match concrete and abstract material, you should be able to satisfy both of these audience demands.

  INTERPRET FACTS: Facts and figures are concrete. If you recite only fact after fact, your audience will grow bored or, worse, confused. You need to provide some analysis and interpretation of the facts for your audience.

  SUPPORT OPINIONS: Ideas, analyses, and interpretations tend to be abstract. If you offer only ideas and opinions, but have no concrete evidence to support your claims, an audience may find you untrustworthy or doubt your conclusions.

- *Information is too general or too specific.* By carefully and consciously moving from the general to the specific and back again, the speaker can introduce variety and improve the audience's chances of seeing both the forest and the trees.

  EXAMPLE: An article about assessing the reliability of an online encyclopedia offers a *general* statement that the task of checking facts and accuracy in an encyclopedia is too huge to do exhaustively or consistently. Not every article can be double and triple checked, so statistical and representative tests are used to verify reliability. The article then goes on to provide a *specific* example, noting that biographical information about Revolutionary War figure Alexander Hamilton offers a useful representative test due to conflicting information about his date of birth.[3]

---

[3] Robert McHenry, "The Faith-Based Encyclopedia," *Tech Central Station* 15 Nov. 2004, 3 May 2005 <http://www.techcentralstation.com/111504A.html>.

Barriers That Involve Audience and Delivery

Four additional barriers to communication involve the circumstances of the presentation and the speaker's style in organizing and delivering the presentation.

- *Audience provides too much or too little feedback.* Because a presentation is primarily a one-way transmission of information, the speaker must find ways to assess whether the audience understands the content of the presentation. You can use a variety of techniques to obtain feedback from your audience— for example, you can watch the reactions of one or two representative members of an audience, or you can pause periodically to invite the audience to ask questions. Of course, if you focus too much on one or two members of an audience, you may lose the focus of your message. On the other hand, too much feedback or too many questions from the audience can disrupt the flow of your presentation or take up valuable time that you need to present your message. You need to balance getting feedback from the audience while keeping your presentation on course.

- *Information is presented too rapidly or too slowly.* Research suggests that "normal conversational delivery" is the best pace for covering material clearly and efficiently. If you talk too quickly or too slowly or do not allow enough time for the audience to absorb your major points, the audience will not be able to understand and retain as much information. Keep in mind that someone reading your paper can backtrack and reread complex points; someone listening to your presentation cannot.

- *Information is presented too soon or too late.* Fortunately, with careful preparation and the knowledge of a few elementary principles of organization, the "too soon/too late" problem is easily solved. For example, by remembering that listeners find it easier to move from the simple to the complex, from the concrete to the abstract, and from the immediate to the anticipated, you can often avoid moving into material too quickly.

Similarly, by knowing that listeners have a need for pattern, chronology, and completeness, you are reminded that information must be "packaged" and organized for an audience to be able to absorb and retain it. (For more about organizing your presentation, see Chapter 5.)

- *Information is presented with too much or too little intensity.* If you get overly involved in the material you are presenting, the audience may feel you are more concerned about preaching or performing than you are about sharing information. On the other hand, if you merely go through the motions without conveying any interest in your topic, the audience will probably share your lack of enthusiasm.

By analyzing your audience and determining their attitudes and expectations, you will be better prepared to overcome potential communication barriers when you deliver your presentation. In the next chapter, you will learn more about choosing the information and evidence that will be most useful and convincing to your specific audience.

Adapting Your Ideas and Evidence   4

In your composition class, written assignments come with specific requirements, one of which may be to present your paper's information orally. Although writing and speaking are related and interdependent, your work is not finished when your paper is written. You may not have time to orally present all of the details in your paper. You need to identify the main ideas that will best help you accomplish the purpose of your presentation and the key evidence that will lead the audience members to accept what you tell them. Remember that you are *presenting* your ideas and scholarship, not *reading* the paper in its entirety.

If you have already written the paper, use the topic sentences of your paragraphs to help you identify main ideas to cover in your presentation. (If you did not create an outline before writing your paper, it's a good idea to do so now.) If you have more than three to five main points to cover in your presentation, consider ways to combine or synthesize the ones that are similar. You also need to decide which pieces of evidence from your paper will be most convincing to your audience of listeners.

Listening and Learning

Your oral presentation probably will present information to your audience that they do not know or that they have only a passing familiarity with. You want them to listen to you and internalize the information you provide. In other words, you want them to learn. You should keep in mind that your presentation is facilitating the audience as they learn new information. The following points may help you relate more effectively to your audience.

- *Individuals have different motivations for learning.* Although "What's in it for me?" and "There might be something of value that I can use" may reflect the bottom-line motivation of audience members, each person has a different motivator. Thus, it is important to build your message on audience analysis.

- *Learning is an individual activity.* The accumulation of knowledge, skills, and attitudes is an experience that occurs within and is activated by the learner. Although you can set the stage and do much to orchestrate a climate conducive to learning, learning is still an internal process.

- *Audience members have prior experiences.* The more you incorporate an audience's life experiences into the construction of a message, the more the audience will retain and use the information provided.

- *Learning results from stimulation to the senses.* An audience member learns better when you appeal to multiple senses. Learners learn best by doing. As Confucius stated it: "I hear and I forget; I see and I remember; I do and I understand."

Choosing Forms of Support

Within a learning framework, then, what specific verbal and nonverbal forms of support can you use to make it easier for the audience to retain and accept your message? Consider the following five forms of support: explanation, examples, statistics, testimony, and visual aids.

Explanation

Explanation is the act or process of making something plain or comprehensible. Providing a definition is one mode of explanation. This alternative can take a variety of forms.

- *Providing a dictionary definition.* Defining typically involves placing the item to be defined in a category and then explaining the features that distinguish the item from all other members of the category—for example, "*Primary* is a word that means 'first in time, order, or importance.'"

- *Using synonyms and/or antonyms.* Synonyms are words with approximately the same meaning—for example, "*Mawkish* as an adjective indicates that someone or something is sentimental, maudlin, or gushy." Antonyms are words that have opposite meanings.

- *Using comparisons and contrasts.* Comparisons show listeners the similarities between something unfamiliar and something familiar. Contrasts emphasize the differences between two things.

- *Defining by etymology (word origin) and history.* For example, "*Pedagogy*, a term used to describe the art and science of teaching children, is derived from the Greek words *paid* meaning 'child,' and *agogus*, meaning 'leader of.'"

- *Providing an operational definition.* An operational definition defines a process by describing the steps involved in that process—for example, "To create calligraphy, you begin with a wide-nibbed pen . . ."

To be effective, explanations must be framed within the experiences of the audience and should not be too long or abstract. You may have explanations in your paper that work well for your presentation as they are. For those that don't, adapt them for listeners—for example, turn a written operational definition into a live demonstration that shows the process to your audience.

Examples

Examples serve as illustrations, models, or instances of what is being explained. An example can be either developed in detail (an illustration) or presented in abbreviated, undeveloped fashion (a specific instance). An illustration—an extended example presented in narrative form—can be either hypothetical (a story that could but did not happen) or factual (a story that did happen). For example, a presenter might involve the listeners in a hypothetical illustration by suggesting, "Imagine yourself getting ready to give an oral presentation. You reach into your bag for the manuscript that you carefully prepared over the course of the past week. It isn't there! You madly search through everything in the bag." Whether hypothetical or factual, an illustration should be relevant and appropriate to the audience, typical rather than exceptional, and vivid and impressive in detail.

A specific instance is an undeveloped or condensed example. It requires listeners to recognize the names, events, or situations in the instance. A presenter, for example, who uses "President Dewey" as a specific instance of the dangers of poor sampling techniques when engaged in public opinion polling must know in advance that the audience will understand that Thomas Dewey was Harry Truman's Republican opponent who was mistakenly announced as the winner in the 1948 presidential election. Otherwise, this example will not make the point clear and vivid and, in fact, probably will confuse or distract the audience.

You may have specific instances in your paper that you can develop further into illustrations so that your audience can get involved and relate to what you are saying. Likewise, you may have illustrations in your paper that you want to mention but not take time to develop in full detail. You could reduce some of those illustrations to specific instances.

Statistics

Statistics describe the end result of collecting, organizing, and interpreting numerical data. They are often presented in graph or table form. Statistics are especially useful when reducing large masses of information to more specific categories, as in the following example accompanied by a bar graph.

◆ Adults who start smoking in their early teens are less likely to quit by age 30 than those who start later. Of those who start after the age of 16, 13.6 percent quit by age 30. But only 9.6

percent of those who start at the ages of 14–15 and 4.4 percent of those who start before age 14 quit by age 30.

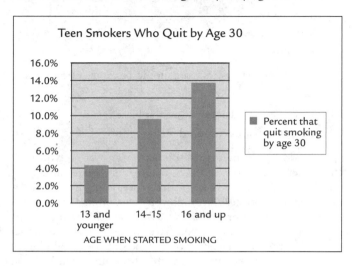

Statistics are also useful for emphasizing the largeness or smallness of something, as in the following example.

♦ Adults spend an average of 16 times as many hours selecting clothes—145.6 hours a year—as on planning for retirement— 9.1 hours a year.

And finally, statistics can describe indications of trends—where we've been and where we're going. The following example describes a trend and summarizes the information in a table.

♦ According to a 1996 survey of 800 newspapers and magazines, 25 percent distributed at least part of their publications electronically. Another 31 percent intended to do so within 2 years; 19 percent intended to do so within 5 years; and 23 percent had no plans to do so.

ELECTRONIC DISTRIBUTION OF NEWSPAPERS AND MAGAZINES IN 1996

Already doing it (at least partially)	25%
Within 2 years	31%
Within 5 years	19%
No plans	23%

When using statistics, you should be aware of two basic concerns:

1. Are the statistics accurate and unbiased?
2. Are the statistics clear and meaningful?

To address the first issue, you need to answer such questions as these: Are the statistical techniques appropriate, and are they appropriately used? Do the statistics cover enough cases and a sufficient length of time? Although you may not have the expertise to answer such questions, you can ask about the credibility of the source of the statistics. Do you have any reason to believe that the person or group from whom you got the statistics might be biased? Are these statistics consistent with other things you know about the situation?

Addressing the second issue involves more pragmatic considerations: Can you translate difficult-to-comprehend numbers into more immediately understandable terms? How in the smoking example, for instance, might you make the difference between 4.4 percent and 13.6 percent more vivid? How can you provide an adequate context for the data? Is it useful in the electronic publishing example, for instance, to put together both newspapers and magazines when exploring use of electronic publication? Is the comparison between planning for retirement and selecting clothing a fair one? Would a graph or visual aid clarify the data and statistical trends? As we will see in Chapter 7, supplementing a verbal presentation with visual aids can greatly increase the audience's comprehension and retention.

If conducted with rigor and proper scientific methodology, statistical research offers useful analysis of trends and potential outcomes. Be certain, though, that you properly cite the source of your statistics and do not rely on "they say" or "experts report." Also, be sure to give the context and scope of the study you cite. One danger of using statistics is the tendency to oversimplify the complexity of the critical question asked in the research study and to downplay the limiting factors that impact the outcomes. For example, a research study may find a statistical link between members of a specific cultural background and left-handedness, but if the study was limited to a test group of art school students, you should be sure to mention that the test group was in art school. You should not assume that the study's findings apply to members of the same cultural group who are interested in engineering or mathematics.

Testimony

Testimony involves using a credible person's statement to lend weight and authority to aspects of your presentation. For this to happen, the person being cited must be qualified; that is, the testimony must come from a person who is an expert on this topic and free of bias and self-interest. Just as important as actual credentials is the perception the audience has of the source of the testimony. Is the individual known to the audience? If not, you will need to tell the audience why the individual is a good authority. If known, is the person accepted by the audience as both knowledgeable and unbiased on the topic? In short, to lend support to a message, the testimony of a source must both be actually credible and be perceived as credible.

For example, recent articles on technology Web sites have debated the value of the online reference site Wikipedia.org. One such article, "The Faith-Based Encyclopedia," critiques not only the reliability of the data in Wikipedia entries, but also the entire notion of accountability within a free online reference written and edited completely by unpaid volunteers. Though the author of the article, Robert McHenry, is an expert on encyclopedias, his bias against the Wikipedia may perhaps be explained (or complicated) by his former position as editor-in-chief of the print edition of *Encyclopaedia Britannica*. Another related article, "Why Wikipedia Must Jettison Its Anti-Elitism," which appeared on the news Web site Kuro5hin.org, appears to be more even-handed in its critique of the Wikipedia; however, the article was written by L. Sanger, one of the founders of the Wikipedia, whose disagreements over how to run the Wikipedia "forked" the project in a new direction into another project called Nupedia. Though Sanger is a reliable source of information about Wikipedia due to his early involvement, his personal reasons for leaving may color and tarnish his objectivity about the subject. Appropriately objective information is found in a third article by technology writer Edward W. Felten, who has no ties to either Britannica or Wikipedia. Together, the three articles offer a number of informed perspectives, but Felten's piece is in many ways more compelling, even though he has no experience in reference writing or editing, either online or in print.

Visual Aids

Visual aids are primarily used to enhance the clarity and credibility of your message. They can also help you control your own nervousness by providing a safety net in an uncertain situation, reminding you of the structure of your presentation and the important points you want to make. Obtaining these advantages requires skill in selecting appropriate aids and using them well. (For more on visual aids, see Chapter 7.)

Choosing Forms of Proof

What motivates the audience to accept your claim about a fact, value, problem, or policy? Since the time of the ancient Greek philosopher Aristotle, forms of proof have been organized into three categories. Aristotle called them *pathos* (motivational proof based on the drives, values, or aspirations of the audience), *ethos* (ethical proof based on the credibility of the source of the message), and *logos* (logical proof based on evidence, such as statistics and examples).

Motivational Proof or Pathos

At the heart of persuasion is the ability to adapt a message to the feelings, needs, and values of an audience. People want and need to interact with others and belong to social groups. They need to feel worthy and to be recognized for their merits. Most, if they have their most basic needs met, develop a desire to grow and achieve their full potential. As you speak, make clear the ways in which your message answers or addresses these needs for the audience. Pathos often involves relating to the audience on a visceral, emotional level. Empathy, which means identifying with and understanding another person's feelings, motivations, or circumstances, shares the same root as *pathos*. If you recognize and anticipate the ways your words will resonate with your audience, you can tie your argument to the emotions you evoke.

In his famous speech, President John F. Kennedy urged Americans to "[a]sk not what your country can do for you. Ask what you can do for your country." By appealing to the traditional work ethic in the American tradition, President Kennedy tapped into an emotional wellspring within the hearts and minds of the public. By using the feelings of responsibility, duty, and even a hint of shame in his stern command that Americans not ask but instead give, Kennedy tied his message to deep, personal feelings in his audience.

Ethical Proof or Ethos

The persuasiveness of a message is commonly assumed to be influenced by the person who delivers it. For example, in social conversations, you may drop the names of respectable sources even as you pass along rumors and gossip. Source credibility—an audience's perception of the speaker separate from the speaker's intent or purpose—is an important factor in whether listeners accept the message. The ethos of a speaker takes into consideration both public reputation and personal standards of conduct. The external evidence of a person's ethical and consistent behavior is one part of ethos. Another is the person's actual behavior, no matter who is watching or what the perceptions of others are. Audiences are confident in a speaker who is known for her deeds, actions, accomplishments, and positions—the letter of the law and evidence of compliance. Speakers gain confidence in themselves by relying on their own morals, responsibilities, and values—the spirit of the law and thoughtful compliance no matter what the repercussions.

Logical Proof or Logos

Logos is one root of any word ending in *-logy*. In Greek, it means "word," but it has come to mean "science," "study," or "theory." *Logical* also comes from *logos*. Appeals to logos involve logical, scientific evidence. We described five verbal and nonverbal devices that you can use to help an audience understand and accept your message: explanations, examples, statistics, testimony, and visual aids. Three of these devices (examples, statistics, and testimony) are especially useful as evidence—that is, information used as logical proof by a speaker. Evidence increases the persuasiveness of a message.[1] As you might expect, highly credible evidence sources are more persuasive than less credible ones. High-quality evidence is especially effective if the audience is unfamiliar with the subject and if the evidence is from multiple sources. Outdated evidence and evidence already familiar to the audience are not as highly persuasive.

To be persuasive, you should use multiple types of evidence. Although research does not suggest that one form of evidence is superior to the others, there is some indication that examples may have greater impact than statistical evidence, perhaps because they create vivid images in the minds of receivers.

Not all sources of information are of equal value, but how can you decide which are more credible than others? In order to evaluate sources, whether you are presenting or listening to a persuasive

[1] John C. Reinard, "The Empirical Study of the Persuasive Effects of Evidence: The Status After Fifty Years of Research," *Human Communication Research* 15 (1988): 3–59.

message, consider the following criteria: Is the source reliable? Recent? Complete? Accurate?[2]

The reliability test holds that sources should be objective and competent. Be skeptical of sources who might have something to gain from promoting a particular point of view. Sources should be in a position to know about the subject at hand, and they should be competent to judge or comment on the specific issue, item, or idea. Strive for the most up-to-date information possible. To meet the completeness criterion, evidence should be based on as many sources as possible. Having multiple sources lets you test the evidence for accuracy. Accurate information is redundant and verifiable. In other words, a variety of sources should present similar information. You should be skeptical of the aberrant figure or idea.

As you choose which ideas and forms of support to include in your presentation, keep in mind that combining different forms of support and forms of proof is often effective. For example, presenting only statistics can result in a dry presentation; presenting only emotional testimony from individuals with no logical evidence can result in an unconvincing presentation. Include in your presentation the same variety of forms of support and proof as in your paper. Balance in both will produce the most persuasive argument possible.

---

[2] Patricia Bradley Andrews, *Basic Public Speaking* (New York: Harper & Row, 1985).

5   *Organizing Your Presentation*

Once you have your statement of purpose, your thesis, and your supporting details, you need to reorganize the ideas in your paper so they are most effective when you make your presentation. When an audience reads a paper, they have the advantages of written text: They can move at their own speed, reread confusing or complicated passages, and look up new vocabulary. In an oral presentation, the audience has few of these options. As a speaker, you have several advantages, however. You can accentuate certain points by altering your tone, volume, or speed, and by gesturing, making eye contact, and using body language. The key task is determining how to translate what you wrote in your paper into a clear, coherent, and effective oral presentation. An outline visually displays the main points and subpoints of your presentation (as well as the support for those points) in a way that helps you develop the presentation.

Creating an Outline

A good strategy for beginning to organize your oral presentation is to turn your paper into a complete sentence outline. Once you have developed such an outline, you may find it useful to reduce it to a topic outline or speaker's outline, which uses brief phrases and keywords in place of sentences. Often presentations do not allow enough time to cover every detail found in the paper. As you outline and organize your presentation, hit all the main points and use examples only sparingly if time is an issue. You may want to include more examples and details in a handout, but speak about only two or three during the presentation.

An outline generally includes several main points (I, II, III, etc.) and at least two subpoints (A, B, etc.) that develop each of the main points. Further subpoints are included for supporting material such as examples, testimony, statistics, and illustrations. In this way, an outline alternates numbers and letters in clearly identifiable columns and can accommodate as many levels of headings as you need. The following example shows a portion of an outline for a presentation on the merits of a popular online encyclopedia:

I. Are free online resources like Wikipedia equal to traditional purchased, print encyclopedias?
   A. What is Wikipedia?
      1. definition of *wiki*
      2. mission statement of Wikipedia.org
   B. What value does online encyclopedia offer?
      1. easy access
      2. current information
      3. multiple volunteer authors
   C. What potential problems?
      1. volunteer status of authors
      2. instability/constant changes
      3. ease of access for uneducated writers and users
         a. writing not of consistent quality
         b. readers not analytical enough
         c. might not be problem, but advantage
II. Wikipedia's reliability . . .

Although the type of labeling used in the above outline is the most common, another popular style is legal-style or decimal-number labeling. The next portion of the sample outline is shown in this style:

2. Wikipedia's reliability

   2.1. Edward W. Felten Sept. 2004 "spot check" of Wikipedia[1]

      2.1.1. checked entries on 6 topics he was well-versed in

      2.1.2. on advice of colleague, checked Britannica online entries same items

   2.2. Sanger, Wikipedia co-founder, on Kuro5hin[2]

      2.2.1. first problem is not how reliable but public's perception of reliability

      2.2.2. acknowledges Wikipedia not reliable for specialized topics, and better sources exist

         2.2.2.1. *Stanford Encyclopedia of Philosophy*

         2.2.2.2. *Internet Encyclopedia of Philosophy*

   2.3. Robert McHenry, former editor-in-chief of *Encyclopaedia Britannica*[3]

      2.3.1. explains fact checking in encyclopedias is similar to Felten's approach

      2.3.2. statistical and representative tests are used . . .

Headings at a particular level of an outline should be of equal importance and written using parallel structure. In the first example, the main points, indicated by roman numerals, are the main divisions of the presentation and are of equal importance. The subpoints

---

[1] Edward W. Felten, "Wikipedia vs. Britannica Smackdown," *Freedom to Tinker* 7 Sept. 2004, 3 May 2005 <http://www.freedom-to-tinker.com/archives/000675.html>.

[2] L. Sanger, "Why Wikipedia Must Jettison Its Anti-Elitism," *Kuro5hin: Technology and Culture, from the Trenches,* 31 Dec. 2004, 3 May 2005 <http://www.kuro5hin.org/story/2004/12/30/142458/25>.

[3] Robert McHenry, "The Faith-Based Encyclopedia," *Tech Central Station,* 15 Nov. 2004, 3 May 2005 <http://www.techcentralstation.com/111504A.html>.

(A, B, and C) also designate equally important divisions of the main point to which they refer. The outline has two or more elements at any level; that is, there are two or more main points, two or more subpoints under any main point, and two or more levels of support. This is normally the case because a topic is not "divided" unless it has at least two parts. If you wish to make only one subpoint, do not show it on the outline as a subpoint but include it as part of the main point.

Choosing an Organizational Pattern

When adapting a paper for an oral presentation, you may need to rearrange the organization of information. What represents a logical progression of ideas in a paper may leave your listeners confused since, unlike readers, they cannot reread passages or look back to important points that preceded. For a presentation, it is often better to provide an overview at the outset, clearly stating which points you intend to cover. Doing so gives your audience a frame of reference that helps them follow and understand your points as you speak. It is sometimes best to cover the most important points first, both because the audience is still fresh and because you have limited time. Alternatively, if you're covering only a few points, you might want to build up to the most important idea so that it remains fresh in the audience's minds after you finish speaking. During your presentation your audience will also rely on you to occasionally summarize or remind them of what you've already covered. The structure of your paper offers a good starting point for organizing your ideas and indeed may be the best structure for your presentation as well. But don't be afraid to experiment with a different pattern of organization for your presentation.

Although you can organize ideas in many ways, the following six organizational patterns are common: chronological, topical, spatial or geographical, cause-effect, problem-solution, and compare and contrast. You will likely already have used at least one of these organizational patterns in your paper.

Chronological Pattern

When using the chronological pattern, you organize your main points in a time-related sequence: that is, forward (or backward) in a systematic fashion. You might, for example, focus on the past, present, and future of digital recording technology. When describing a process step by step, you are also using a chronological pattern. The following terms make good transitions in a chronological pattern:

first . . .	next . . .	afterwards . . .
to begin . . .	before you continue . . .	eventually . . .
at the outset . . .	when that is completed . . .	finally . . .

Topical Pattern

Also known as a categorical pattern, the topical pattern organizes the main points as parallel elements of the topic itself. Perhaps the most common way of organizing a presentation, the topical pattern is useful when describing components of persons, places, things, or processes. A secondary concern when selecting this approach is the sequencing of topics. Depending on the circumstances, this is often best handled in ascending or descending order—that is, according to the relative importance, familiarity, or complexity of the topics. The example that follows begins with a specific question about a particular online resource and progresses to more complex questions about the reliability of online resources in general.

I.   Are free online resources like Wikipedia equal to traditional purchased, print encyclopedias?

II. Wikipedia's reliability is a question of both real and perceived accuracy.

III. Can some solution be achieved, or are critics just complaining without offering to help?

IV. Is the question of reliability in online resources really a problem? Why?

Spatial or Geographical Pattern

The spatial or geographical pattern arranges main points in terms of their physical proximity to or direction from each other (north to south, east to west, bottom to top, left to right, near to far, outside to inside, and so on). It is most useful when explaining objects, places, or scenes in terms of their component parts.

Cause-Effect Pattern

With the cause-effect pattern, you attempt to organize the message around cause-to-effect or effect-to-cause relationships. That is, you might move from a discussion of the origins or causes of a phenomenon, say increases in the cost of fuel, to the eventual results or effects, such as increases in the cost of airplane tickets. Or, you could move from a description of present conditions (effects) to an identification and description of apparent causes. The choice of strategy is often based on which element—cause or effect—is more familiar to the intended audience. The cause-effect pattern of organization is especially useful when your purpose is to achieve understanding or agreement, rather than action, from the recipients of a message.

Problem-Solution Pattern

The problem-solution pattern involves dramatizing an obstacle and then narrowing alternative remedies to the one that you recommend. Thus, the main points of a message are organized to show that (1) there is a problem that requires a change in attitude, belief, or behavior; (2) a number of possible solutions might solve this problem; and (3) your solution is the one that will most effectively and efficiently provide a remedy. Topics that lend themselves to this organizational pattern include a wide range of business, social, economic, and political problems for which you can propose a workable solution. The problem-solution pattern of organization is especially useful when the purpose of a message is to generate audience action.

Compare and Contrast Pattern

One of the most common assignments (and most commonly misunderstood assignments) is a comparison paper or compare and contrast paper. Comparing is the act of identifying similarities, the characteristics shared by two or more distinct items or topics. Contrasting is identifying differences, the characteristics not shared by those items or topics. If your instructor assigns this type of presentation, be sure you understand whether you are supposed to compare only, contrast only, or both. Ask questions if you are unsure.

Patterns of Organization
Chronological organization
I want my audience to know that building a new student center on campus is a complex process.
<ul><li>Gain approval of board of trustees</li><li>Garner community support</li><li>Raise additional funds</li><li>Work with architects, engineers, consultants, and contractors</li><li>Anticipate and solve problems caused by construction</li></ul>
Topical organization
I want my audience to know that there are three major issues for the college to consider before deciding whether to build a new student center.
<ul><li>The cost of the project</li><li>The short-term problems associated with the project</li><li>The potential long-term benefits of the project</li></ul>
Spatial organization
I want my audience to know that the proposed student center will have four main areas.
<ul><li>Café</li><li>Game room</li><li>Computer lab</li><li>Club offices</li></ul>
Cause-effect organization
I want my audience to know that campuses with good student centers have a better sense of community among the student body.
<ul><li>*Cause:* Good student center</li><li>*Effect:* Greater sense of community</li></ul>

Problem-solution organization

I want my audience to know that a problem associated with building a new student center is lack of funds for the project, and that the problem can be solved by using more effective fundraising techniques.

- *Problem:* Lack of funds
- *Solution:* Better fundraising techniques
- *Advantage:* Increased income for the project

Comparison organization

I want my audience to know that the new student center and the existing athletic center will be similar in three ways.

- Open to all students
- Appeals to incoming applicants
- Provides work-study job opportunities for students

Contrast organization

I want my audience to know that the new student center and the existing athletic center will be different in two ways.

- *Student center:* Open to students only; no classes meet there
- *Athletic center:* Open for paid public use during certain hours; some required courses meet there

---

Writers and speakers rarely use only one structure in the course of a paper or oral presentation. Effective speakers tend to use more complex combinations of several patterns to develop each main point of an oral presentation, as illustrated in the following partial outline.

There are three major issues for the college to consider before deciding whether to build a new student center on campus:

I. The cost-effectiveness of the project   TOPICAL

    A. Not enough money in the current budget to fund the project

       PROBLEM-SOLUTION

    B. Enough funds can be attained through better fundraising techniques

      1. Special campaign to target recent alumni

      2. Joint fundraising efforts with clubs and other student organizations on campus   TOPICAL

II. The short-term problems associated   TOPICAL
with the project
   A. An unsightly construction site
   B. Detours and traffic flow problems   CAUSE-EFFECT
      along the main campus road
   C. Potential security risks
III.   The potential long-term benefits of   TOPICAL
       the project . . .

Once you have determined the overall pattern of organization for your presentation, examine each main point in your outline. On the basis of each point, choose appropriate subpatterns for developing your ideas. If ideas fall naturally into a particular pattern of organization, do not force them into some other pattern; develop whatever combination of patterns works best for your ideas and achieves your purpose.

Developing Effective Introductions, Transitions, and Conclusions 6

Composing a paper (at least a good paper!), is a process, one in which you discover new ideas, and new ways to organize your ideas, as you write. After writing a first draft, for example, you may find that your thesis statement isn't as clear or as narrowly focused as you intended. Or perhaps you decide that your thesis statement needs stronger supporting points. You may find too that your conclusion needs to be summarized or restated. Writers who compose strong and persuasive papers regularly use all of these strategies.

Another part of the composing process involves choosing words and transitions. All the information in your paper needs connective words and phrases that link your points together into one cohesive and coherent argument. Rethinking their word choices during writing of second drafts is common among strong writers.

All of the composition principles true for writing papers are also true for making oral presentations. You need to write an introduction and a conclusion, and tie the sections of your presentation together with transitions.

The Introduction

When you give an oral presentation outside of class, the setting or the person introducing you may have already provided an overview of your message. Your audience may be so fired up about the topic that motivating them to listen to you is not necessary. Maybe your credibility as a speaker on the topic is so high that it does not require additional development. For most of your presentations in class, however, this is not the case. To compensate, you need to provide an overview of your message, motivate your audience to pay attention, and establish your credibility as a speaker on the topic.

Your introduction often is the most important part of the presentation. You must be clear, concise, and efficient when beginning your presentation in order to keep your audience's attention and prepare them for your message. Writing your introduction last, after you have written the rest of your paper or presentation, is often a good strategy because doing so gives you the opportunity to prepare your audience for all the main points you will cover. Keep in mind that your audience cannot refer back to your introduction in the same way they can when reading a paper. Refer back to your main points at strategic times throughout your presentation.

When you get up to speak, your audience probably has questions: What will this presentation be like? Will I like and trust this speaker? What will I get out of listening to this presentation? A good introduction answers these and other important questions. Dedicate about 5 to 10 percent of your speaking time to answering questions like these about your intent, the audience's relationship to both you and to the material, and the importance of this presentation to their lives or ways of thinking.

Although there is no guaranteed approach to making your intentions clear, consider explicitly stating the topic, thesis, title, or purpose. Previewing the structure of the message ("The three points I will develop are . . .") may be another useful plan. You may also want to explain why you narrowed the topic down from something more complex or involved.

A good way to motivate your audience to listen is to link your topic and thesis to their lives. Showing how the topic has, does, or will affect the audience's past, present, or future will help gain their interest and investment. You may also succeed in gaining the interest of your audience by demonstrating how the topic is linked to a basic need or goal, of either people in general or this audience specifically. Make the audience feel important through your introduction; show the audience how important they are in your details and supporting information.

Of course, you need to motivate your audience and build your credibility throughout your presentation, not only in your introduction. Many of the ways to build credibility are similar to those you use in writing a paper; however, when you are speaking in front of an audience, you are also communicating your credibility and trustworthiness through your body language and your ability to connect with the audience. Strategies for building credibility include the following.

- Cite highly credible individuals and reliable sources.

  ◆ "Robert McHenry, former editor-in-chief of *Encyclopaedia Britannica,* has written . . ."

  ◆ "In a speech from his hospital bed, Ambassador Morris B. Abram, a lawyer, educator, civil rights activist, and diplomat, has said that 'the question of treatment . . . should be based not on the length of time from birth but on the length of time from death.' "[1]

- Place your topic in historical context.

  ◆ "Since the advent of digital music technology, especially the CD in the 1980s and the mp3 in the 1990s, . . ."

  ◆ "Before the advent of the World Wide Web, this discussion would not have made sense. In fact, even as recently as 2000, the topic of a publicly edited free encyclopedia would have sounded more like a dream than reality to most people."

- Describe your personal acquaintance with the topic.

  ◆ "I was an early adopter of Napster, and after legal problems changed their business model, I switched to Morpheus and KaZaa."

[1] Morris B. Abram, "Some Views on Ethics and Later Life," *Controversies in Ethics in Long-Term Care,* ed. Ellen Olson, Eileen R. Chichin, and Leslie S. Libow (New York: Springer, 1995) 146.

- ◆ "My parents both have living wills, and I, myself, am an organ donor, as you can see by this symbol on my driver's license."

- Entertain alternative points of view to show that you are speaking from a balanced perspective.
- Be sure your body language supports what you claim to think and feel about your topic.
- Be gracious and polite with your audience, even if they seem hostile to your message.
- Use relevant humor, if appropriate, to demonstrate that both you and your listeners laugh at the same things.

The introduction to your presentation need not accomplish all of these goals. However, many opening strategies can function in multiple ways, allowing you to state your topic, establish a connection with the audience, and begin to demonstrate your credibility. For example, a story or an analogy can do all three of those things—"The reason I am so impassioned about end-of-life care is readily summed up in this story about my grandmother. . . ." Humor can both emphasize your motivation for making the presentation and help develop a better relationship between you and the audience. The best advice is to make your introduction as brief as possible while fulfilling the audience's expectations concerning what you want to do, how you relate to them, and why you feel the way you do about the topic.

Language Choices

When you begin to think through how best to convey the main ideas of a message, it is imperative that you examine your word and language choices; the best choices make your message relevant, clear, and unbiased for audience members. Here are some guidelines that can help you achieve this goal for your oral presentation.

- *Public language should be personal.* Don't borrow someone else's vocabulary. Use language that you can use easily. Never use a word in an oral presentation that you haven't said out loud previously. Practice pronouncing a new word until you make it yours.

- *Public language should be fitting.* Listen carefully to the language patterns of your listeners before you speak to them. Adjust the formality of your language to fit the situation. Resist the temptation to use a pet phrase just because you like it. Don't be flip with a serious topic or melodramatic with a light one.

    ◆ **APPROPRIATE WORD CHOICE FOR A RESIDENCE HALL FLOOR MEETING:** "So we have to stop leaving a mess in the bathroom, know what I'm saying? You can't be leaving surprises for the janitors, you feel me?"

    ◆ **MORE APPROPRIATE LANGUAGE FOR A CLASS PRESENTATION:** "The defacement of public property on campus is the responsibility of the entire campus community, as I am sure you will agree."

- *Public language should be strategic.* If you're dealing with touchy topics or hostile listeners, try out several different ways of phrasing a volatile idea in order to achieve the right tone. Don't depend on the inspiration of the moment to guide your language choice. Think in advance about what you're going to say and how you're going to say it. Compare the tone of the following three examples.

    ◆ "The ROTC needs to get off campus now."

    ◆ "The college needs to expel the recruiters immediately."

    ◆ "While the military offers a number of benefits to recruits as far as job placement and tuition support, perhaps the time has come for the administration of this university to examine its policies regarding on-campus recruiting."

- *Public language should be oral.* Except in certain rare circumstances, do not read your presentation; instead, make your presentation in an expository fashion. An oral presentation is meant for the ear, not the eye. Listen to the words and phrases you intend to use. Put "catch phrases" in your outline rather than long, elaborate sentences. Use your voice and body to signal irony and rhetorical questions and to emphasize important points. And practice reading your presentation at least several times, ideally with a friend or family member as a test audience.

- *Public language should be precise.* If you're talking about bulldozers, don't call them *earth-moving vehicles.* As in a paper, avoid unnecessary jargon and define all technical terms for your listeners. Try to avoid vague generalities; instead, use concrete and specific language when providing descriptions.

- *Public language should be simple.* Readers have an easier time understanding complicated sentences than listeners do. When speaking, use simple sentences as often as possible, and use five-syllable words sparingly.

- *Public language should be unaffected.* Don't seek to have your listeners remember your language. Don't get carried away with metaphors; a single simple image is always superior to several complex ones. Don't invent "cute" phrases. Euphemistic language often sounds ludicrous or evasive (for example, referring to firing employees as *downsizing*).[2]

Transitions

Transitions guide an audience through your presentation. They are signs that tell the audience where you are, where you are going, and where you have been. Thus, they need to be overt, clear, and frequent. You might, for example, preview the structure of the message toward the end of the introduction ("Today, I will talk about five behaviors that characterize effective leaders. They are . . ."). Overt tactics like this ground your message for the audience and maintain the context of the information.

[2] Robert P. Hart, Gustav W. Friedrich, Barry Brummet, *Public Communication,* 2nd ed. (New York: Harper & Row, 1983) 170–171.

Informative presentations benefit from direct and overt descriptions and lists. Persuasive arguments may also benefit from such directness, but more subtle transitions are often more useful and reveal a greater degree of sophistication. Sometimes it is enough to put the elements of your presentation in the proper order and then allow your audience to arrive at the same conclusions without you telling them what comes next. Be sure, though, that you move from point to point in a logical fashion, and that you occasionally remind your audience of the thesis, topic, or main idea.

As the presentation proceeds, you can use internal previews and summaries to review a main point and anticipate the next one ("Having described why leaders need to challenge the process, let's turn now to the need to inspire a shared vision"). Sequential terms like *First . . ., Next . . ., And finally . . .* help tie points together. Too-frequent use of these types of transitions, however, can make your presentation sound clinical or sterile, like a user manual or cookbook.

Occasional use of coordinating conjunctions (such as *and, but,* and *or*), correlative conjunctions (such as *either . . . or, not only . . . but also*) and similar grammatical constructions often alleviates the "step-by-step" feel. Use *further* or *furthermore* to enhance certain points and build on previous information. *Again* can accomplish a similar goal. A semicolon (in the written outline) followed by *however* can introduce another perspective and reveal the depth of your research and the degree of your objectivity. Be certain that you use these constructions correctly, and don't overuse the same one. Starting every sentence with "*However . . .*" or "*Though . . .*" quickly grows boring. Check your writing guide or handbook for advice on making smooth transitions in your paper; many of the same techniques work well in a presentation. Remember, however, that you need to summarize and even repeat points more frequently in speaking than in writing.

The Conclusion

A conclusion typically summarizes the main points of the presentation and reinforces the importance of the message by demonstrating its potential impact. An effective way to accomplish this is by using the conclusion to elaborate on an example, illustration, or quotation that was used in the introduction. The conclusion might include a final summary that revisits your transitions ("I've talked today about five behaviors that characterize effective leaders. Effective leaders . . .").

The introduction and conclusion of your presentation act as a frame or set of bookends for your message. As you write the conclusion, consider your introduction carefully. Has your presentation covered all the material you mention in your introduction? Is your thesis statement or main idea supported by the details in the presentation? If you have a rough outline but have not written the details of the presentation, try writing your conclusion first. The conclusion then becomes a target toward which you aim as you compose the presentation. You may want to write more than one conclusion. The one you decide *not* to use as a conclusion may be a good model for your introduction.

Visual aids are useful tools for presentations both because they help sustain the audience's interest and because they deliver certain types of information in a more potent or easily understood way than speaking does alone. Charts, graphs, outlines, and even props for a demonstration are all types of visuals. They can be displayed by using slides, overhead transparencies, handouts, or other methods, such as drawing on a whiteboard or chalkboard. Using visual aids requires careful planning to decide what information is best suited for visual display. You may find yourself tempted to load your presentation with lots of visuals in an attempt to entertain or impress your audience, but too many visuals—or too much information on each visual—can be confusing. A visual aid should never distract but instead help your audience follow your presentation while keeping them focused on what you are saying. Above all else, do not spend more time developing your visual aids than you spend researching and writing your presentation.

Choosing Effective Visuals

A powerful tactic for persuading an audience or demonstrating a task is to show an example. Telling your audience about your topic but never actually showing them what you are describing limits their ability to grasp and internalize the situation or problem. For example, if you are discussing Impressionist painters and paintings, imagine the difference between describing several paintings and displaying those paintings on a screen or in color handouts. Or, suppose you are discussing how a particular writer's childhood experiences influenced his or her later work. You might show the audience a photograph of the writer's hometown to help them imagine the environment. Similarly, medical or scientific presentations benefit greatly from photographs or diagrams, particularly when different items are being compared. For example, for a presentation on different methods of fruit farming, you might use photographs or even bring in several types of apples or oranges to show differences in their growth based on the farming methods used.

Certain types of visuals are more effective than others for certain purposes. Photographs and drawings are especially useful for illustrating a description of an object, a person, or a place. For showing steps in a process, flowcharts, live demonstrations using props, or demonstrations on video are useful. Video clips that show events or provide quotes in a source's own voice reinforce your message both visually and aurally. Showing a written outline of your presentation helps the audience keep track of your main points and follow your line of argument.

Charts and graphs work especially well for displaying statistics, survey results, or other kinds of numerical information. Presenting complex data in visual form through a chart or graph helps your listeners more quickly process, retain, and compare the information. Keeping track of numbers is usually difficult for the audience, but a chart or graph offers them the chance to more clearly comprehend your data and its significance. If possible, use color or distinct markings in your graphs. Label the data clearly, using a key at the side of the chart or with clearly legible units and labels. (For examples of charts and graphs, see the section on statistics in Chapter 4.)

Always use caution and judgment regarding the appropriateness and practicality of your examples. Bringing a live animal to the classroom may be more effective than showing photographs, but it may not be safe or practical! Ask your instructor if you are uncertain about the examples you have chosen. In addition, be sure to cite your source for any visuals you use. If you create a visual such as a chart or graph yourself, cite your source for the information that the chart or graph displays.

Choosing a Mode of Delivery

Whatever type of visuals you choose, you have several options for displaying them to your audience. You can write or draw them on a chalkboard or whiteboard, print them on paper to hand out to the audience, display them onscreen using a projector, or use some combination of these methods. Each method has its own advantages and disadvantages, so you need to consider carefully your purpose, your audience's needs, the equipment available, and the physical setup of the room where you will be presenting.

Chalkboard or Whiteboard

One of the simplest ways to illustrate a point or to show your audience a basic graphic is to write or draw it on a chalkboard or whiteboard at the front of the room. Nearly every classroom has a chalkboard or whiteboard, and you won't need to waste time setting up any special equipment. For illustrating just a few points for a small audience, a chalkboard or whiteboard works well. However, if you are presenting in a large room or need to show extensive or complicated visual examples, a chalkboard or whiteboard is probably not your best choice.

Handouts

Handouts are useful for oral presentations for many reasons:

- A handout provides written information, such as an outline or quotes, to reinforce the content and organization of your message.

- A handout allows the audience to see spellings of difficult terms or definitions of unfamiliar jargon.

- A handout gives the audience a place to take notes and tie their comments and questions to specific portions of your presentation.

- A handout provides a bibliography so that your audience can follow up on any sources that strike their interest.

- A handout shows detailed charts, graphs, or visuals more legibly than a projected onscreen image will.

- A handout gives the audience something to take home as a reminder of your message.

Handouts have disadvantages as well. If you distribute a handout at the beginning of your presentation, the audience may spend their time reading the handout instead of listening to you. The time the audience spends looking down at the handout means fewer opportunities for you to make eye contact and connect with your audience. Sometimes audience members think they don't need to pay attention at all because they can read the handout later. And in a large classroom or lecture hall, distributing handouts to everyone may take too much time away from your presentation. Distributing handouts at the end of the presentation avoids some of these problems but deprives the audience of the opportunity to take notes on or refer to the handout. You may want to ask a classmate to distribute the handouts for you at an appropriate time during your presentation, but this, too, is distracting. You need to decide whether the benefits of using a handout outweigh the disadvantages in your particular situation.

If you choose to create a handout, be sure to make it concise and relevant. Do not give every member of your audience a typed copy of your presentation; instead, use your outline as a starting point and include only the major points and most important details. Significant examples and support should appear on the handout, as should citations for the most relevant and useful research sources you consulted for your paper or presentation. Be sure to include the title of your presentation and your name. You may also want to include the name of the course, the semester, the date, or your e-mail address so that the audience can contact you later with any questions.

Overhead Transparencies

Overhead projectors allow you to display transparencies on a screen. Transparencies are clear sheets of plastic film on which you can print information. Opaque projectors are used in a similar way but can display information from opaque sheets of paper. By using overheads, you display information legibly to a large audience and keep the audience's attention focused on you and your message as you speak. You can point to particular images or evidence, or even write on overheads with a marker during your presentation to make visual links between ideas and examples.

Overheads should display simplified versions of your information. While a single handout could outline your entire presentation, multiple overhead transparencies can break up that information over several screens and help organize subtopics within your presentation. Transparencies also offer you flexibility because you can easily go back to a previous transparency to revisit a point, overlay transparencies to build up an idea, or change the order if you are short on time and need to skip something.

One of the disadvantages of using transparencies is that you have to load each one onto the projector by hand. For this reason, too many transparencies can easily lead to confusion or fumbling. You'll have enough to concern you during the presentation, so try to limit the number of transparencies you use. Three or four transparencies to cover your main subtopics, along with one as an overview, is plenty. If you plan to show charts or examples, it may be best to have one overview transparency and a transparency for each chart or example. You can also put more than one example or section on the same transparency and cover one or the other with a sheet of paper until time for display. Attaching sticky notes or colored tabs to your transparencies also helps with organization and quick switching.

Presentation Software

Presentation software allows you to create slides and display them onscreen with a computer projector, which avoids many of the problems of using transparencies and overhead projectors. Most computers come equipped with a basic version of at least one presentation software package; Microsoft PowerPoint, Open Office Present, and Apple Keynote are just three brands of this software.

The main advantage to presentation software packages is that they allow the mingling of a variety of delivery modes. Most presentation software allows you to include text, digital graphics, screen shots, and other elements within your slides. These types of programs allow you to quickly and easily create polished and professional slide presentations. Unlike overhead transparencies, they allow smooth and speedy transitions from one slide or image to another. Most of these programs also make it easy to create handouts for your audience because you can print out your slides, as shown in Screen 1, or print out a selected number of slides per page, as shown in screens 2 and 3. Most programs also allow you to print "notes pages," which include extra space with each slide for adding handwritten notes.

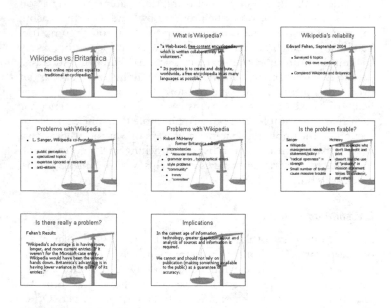

Screen 1: Presentation slides

Screen 2: Printing handouts

Screen 3: Selecting the number of slides per handout

A common mistake that speakers make in creating presentation slides is loading each slide with too much information. Slides work well for reminding the audience of your main points, signaling transitions, and displaying important graphics. But you, not your slides, are giving the presentation. Your audience does not need to see all of your information and examples on slides because you are there to explain the information. Your slides need only include general overviews, main points, and significant graphics or examples. Complete sentences are not necessary where a single word or a concise phrase will do. Do not read your slides directly from the screen because doing so faces you away from the audience. Feel free to approach the screen to point or gesture to a chart or graph, but remember that the slides are there for the audience's benefit, not to take your place. Any visual aid, and particularly presentation slides, should help your audience follow your presentation while keeping them focused on what you are saying. If you plan to do an electronic presentation, spend ample time developing it and practicing with the software.

Designing Visual Aids

Whether you are designing handouts, transparencies, or presentation slides, keep things simple. Visual aids should not repeat every word in your outline or your original paper; they need only present a skeleton or thumbnail sketch of the most important details or visuals. As the speaker, you will fill in the remaining details. Limit the amount of text you include, and use bulleted or numbered lists to keep the material concise. Try to limit handouts to one or two pages, double-sided if you use two pages. For slides and transparencies, "less is more." The focus of your presentation should be the words you say and how you say them, not what's happening over your shoulder.

Fonts

Stick to conventional fonts such as Times, Arial, Palatino, and Helvetica for the main body text, and use display fonts (those that look like band logos, dripping liquids, or other exotic components) only for the heading of the page or slide, if at all. Make sure the text is readable. For a transparency or slide that is projected onscreen, a 24-point font is generally the minimum size that your audience will be able to see from a distance; use even larger type if you can. Sans-serif fonts are easier for audiences to read on a screen. (Serifs are the small extensions on letters in certain fonts, as shown in the examples below. Sans-serif fonts do not have serifs.)

Recommended Serif Fonts	*Recommended Sans-Serif Fonts*	*Display or Headline Fonts*
Times	Arial	**Futura Bold**
Palatino	Verdana	*Monotype Corsiva*

Contrast and Spacing

As you consider design, pay attention to negative space and contrast. Negative space is the (usually white) unfilled portion of the page or screen. Do not cram too many items and words into the small space. Leave room for your information to "breathe." You want your audience to be able to quickly and comfortably access the information you project or hand out. Contrast is the degree of difference in thickness, darkness, or complexity of your text. The headings on this page are set in boldface because that boldness offers a contrast to the normal text on the page, making the heading stand out. The heading also stands out because of the amount of white space surrounding it. For another example, look at the contrast in the title slide of a presentation:

Wikipedia vs. Britannica
Are free online resources equal to traditional encyclopedias?

The first line of text is set in a serif font set in italics with conventional capitalization. The second line, the subtitle, uses a smaller sans-serif font set in boldface with no capitalization. Note that although this example uses several contrasting elements, it still uses fonts that are easy to read.

Color

Use very few colors in your design—two is probably enough; three is likely too many. Stick to basic colors and avoid those that are too bright or have a neon effect. If you are designing presentation slides, either light text on a very dark background or dark text on a very light background works well. Be especially cautious when using the ready-made slide templates that most presentation software packages include—not all of them are well designed.

Be judicious as well in using special features such as animation and sound effects in presentation slides. Most animation is distracting and most sound effects are unnecessary during a presentation. The first time a slide transitions to the next with an explosion or a flash of laser light is surprising and maybe interesting. The fifth time is neither.

Images

One or two meaningful and well-chosen images help reinforce your message, but avoid adding meaningless clip art or excessive decoration. In the following overview slide from a presentation on film piracy, the image of the ticket reinforces the topic by boldly claiming "ADMIT ONE," drawing a link between film piracy and the price of admission. The

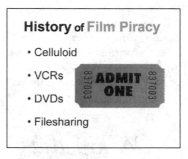

Overview slide

image suits the topic and adds to the message more so than, say, a clip art image of a movie camera or a director's chair. Note as well that plenty of white space surrounds the image and text. The bulleted list uses single words, rather than sentences, to point out main subpoints of the presentation.

Avoiding Technical Problems

Before you devote time to creating visual aids, make sure that the classroom where you will be presenting has the equipment you need. You may need to request or reserve a projector in advance. If you are using presentation software or displaying other files with an LCD (liquid crystal display) projector, check to be sure that your software and all of your files will work on the computer you'll be using during the presentation. (HTML, JPG, GIF, RTF, and PDF files work best with the widest variety of computers and operating systems.)

Computer media can be unreliable, so save multiple copies of all your visual aids in different locations. Copy your handout and your software presentation on more than one disk. Burn a CD-ROM or copy the file to a flash drive. E-mail the presentation to yourself. Save the file on the hard drive of the computer you will use for the presentation (if you are permitted to do so) a day or more before the due date. If doing a group presentation, give every member of the group a copy of the files. Know the size of your audience in advance so that you can print enough handouts, and always bring extra handouts to the presentation. Finally, always have a Plan B, and if you have time and resources, have a Plan C.

Practicing, Polishing, and Delivering the Presentation

Good speakers thoroughly plan both the content of their presentations and their style of delivery. Although it is fundamental to have a clear and logical message to present, that message must be presented effectively. Otherwise, the only person who will understand and accept it is the speaker. Once you have prepared an effective message, you must develop effective strategies to deliver it. Your mode of speaking and your voice, body language, and comfort level all have a significant effect on your audience.

Modes of Speaking

Presentations involve any of four modes of speaking: impromptu, extemporaneous, scripted, or memorized.

Impromptu Speaking

Impromptu speaking is done on the spur of the moment without any formal preparation. By definition, this kind of speaking is not the kind you will be doing if you are preparing an oral presentation for class. But you are likely to be called on to do this type of speaking in other situations, for example, in a classroom setting in which the teacher asks you to summarize and give your opinion of the most recent reading assignment, or in a committee meeting in which you have special expertise on the topic at hand. You cannot prepare your exact words in advance, but you can anticipate the situation and prepare your ideas. When you are asked to answer a question or describe something on the spur of the moment, do the following.

- Quickly identify why you are speaking (for example, to supply needed information, to urge action, to clarify an issue, to provide humor).

  - "In order to defend the position that online reference works such as Wikipedia are sometimes more useful than traditional encyclopedias . . ."

  - "What are the real issues at the heart of the debate over Digital Rights Management and downloading music? I will offer a brief list of concerns . . ."

- Use an organizational strategy (for example, chronological, cause-effect, problem-solution).

  - "Before the early days of the movie industry, film piracy was usually a matter of theft and copying the actual film stock . . . The development of the VCR in the 1970s changed the way the film industry thought about piracy . . . Recent technology like TiVo and the DVD have once again changed perspectives about copyright infringement . . ."

- Grab the audience's attention and relate the core of your message in your introduction.

  - "I get angry every time I pay $10 to see a film at a movie theater and have to sit through a public service announcement warning me not to copy and trade movies because I will put all the members of the film crew out of work. Maybe you have felt this way, too. We paid for this movie! Why are they preaching at us?"

- Speak briefly. If you ramble on, the audience will miss your point.

- When in doubt, summarize. A quick review often restores your perspective and gets you back on track.

  - "I have explained Mr. Sanger's involvement in creating the Wikipedia. I have also detailed Mr. McHenry's former employment with *Encyclopaedia Britannica*. These roles are significant because . . ."

- ◆ "So, licensing is a complicated issue. As I said originally, the owners of copyrighted material and the companies that distribute that material are often working from a different perspective than we, the customers, are. While we believe that we own a song or movie, as I have discussed, they believe that they have only licensed a copy of the performance or film for us to use in our homes. You can see why copying and playing those performances is such a complex subject . . ."

- Finish up with a brief summary stating the outcomes of accepting your message.

    - ◆ "If you want to see better quality free resources, you will have to be conscientious, both as a reader and as a writer. Rather than complaining like Robert McHenry about problems with online resources, we need to read them carefully. Analysis is the most important skill we can learn and use in the current age of information technology. When we see problems, it is up to us to make changes and take part—to give back. I hope what I have said today will make two things clear—that information is not true just because we see it in print, whether online or in a book, and that we have a responsibility to double-check and help correct the information we find online."

- Whatever you do, don't apologize—for your lack of preparation, your lack of information, or your lack of ability as a speaker.

Extemporaneous Speaking

Extemporaneous speaking is characterized by advance preparation of ideas and supporting material, with the precise wording to be composed at the moment of speaking. As a result, no matter how many times the presentation is delivered, the expression of the ideas is never exactly the same. Extemporaneous speaking has a number of important advantages.

- It allows the speaker to adapt to unforeseen situations (for example, by adding a reference to something that occurred in the setting and adding or deleting an argument based on audience response).

- It promotes a more personal relationship between the speaker and the audience.

- It leads, with experience, to a superior delivery—greater earnestness, greater sincerity, and greater power.

Because of these advantages, extemporaneous speaking is the preferred mode of speaking for most situations. Extemporaneous speakers construct a detailed outline and reduce it to a speaker's outline. (For more about outlining, see Chapter 5.) Using the speaker's outline, the speaker rehearses the presentation in front of a mirror, an audio- or video-recorder, and/or helpful friends. During the presentation, the speaker watches the audience for clues about how they are receiving the message and modifies the presentation based on that feedback.

Scripted Speaking

Although extemporaneous is the preferred mode of delivery for most situations, some occasions require you to write out a speech word for word and read the resulting document to the audience. Situations that require or encourage scripted speaking are those for which precision of expression is crucial. When the president of the United States makes a major policy statement on an important issue, he wants to be sure that the wording of the statement will not be misunderstood. Thus, he (or a speech writer) is likely to write out that statement and read it. Scripted speaking is also encouraged in situations that require precise timing (for example, a 2-minute speech written for inclusion in a political commercial).

Preparing a scripted presentation involves the same process as preparing an extemporaneous presentation. That is, you start with a detailed outline, reduce it to a speaker's outline, and rehearse from this outline. (For more about outlining, see Chapter 5.) Once you have experimented with a conversational style for presenting the message, write it down word for word and then rehearse and rewrite, rehearse and rewrite. Once in final form, the scripted presentation is prepared for easy reading—that is, put in a format and type size that are easy to read and marked appropriately to indicate any special emphases. The following example shows an excerpt from a scripted presentation.

♦ "If you want to see better quality free resources, you will have to be conscientious, [*pause*] both as a reader and as a writer. Rather than complaining about problems with online resources, we need to read them carefully. Analysis is the most <u>important</u> skill we can learn and use in the current age of information technology. When <u>we see problems</u>, it is up to <u>us</u> to make changes and take part—[*pause*] to give back. I hope what I have said today will make two things clear—[*pause*] that information is not true just because we see it in print, whether online or in a book, [*pause*] and that we have a responsibility to <u>double-check</u> and <u>help correct</u> the information we find online."

When presenting a scripted oral presentation, you attempt to establish a level of contact with the audience that approaches that of the extemporaneous mode, including steady eye contact and a conversational style of delivery.

Memorized Speaking

Memorized speaking adds one step to a scripted presentation: After writing out the manuscript, you memorize the presentation and then deliver it from memory rather than reading it. In many situations, speakers combine these two approaches: They read parts of the manuscript and deliver other parts of the message from memory in an extemporaneous fashion. In some situations, however, speakers make the extra effort of memorizing the whole document, especially for ceremonial speeches such as tributes and eulogies. When speakers make a special effort to memorize a presentation, they also make a special effort to deliver it using a style of delivery that is as close to an extemporaneous style of delivery as possible. Such a style is best developed by observing the skills of effective speakers, learning to evaluate your own delivery, and practicing to improve your skills.

Voice and Body Language

Once you have chosen a mode of delivery, you next need to consider how to use delivery to focus attention on the message and not on you. This means delivering the message in a conversational style that the audience can both hear and understand. Chapter 3 covers the following potential barriers to effective communication with your audience:

- The amount of information you include
- The type of information you include
- The level of feedback from the audience
- The pace of the presentation
- Organization and timing
- The intensity with which you present the information

As you practice your presentation, you need to consider two other factors that affect the audience—your vocal delivery and your body language.

Whether you are speaking extemporaneously or from a script, speak loudly enough, slowly enough, and clearly enough for the audience members at the back of the room to hear and understand you. If you have the opportunity to practice your presentation in the room where you will be presenting, ask a friend to sit at the back of the room to test whether you are speaking loudly enough. Nervousness may tempt you to rush through your presentation, and you may end up speaking faster than you think you do. Slow down and pause between major points so that your audience has time to absorb what you're saying. Take care to pronounce your words clearly and to speak in a natural, conversational style. Finally, avoid using distracting filler words such as *uh, um, like,* and *you know.* A brief pause is often more effective for helping you get your thoughts together without distracting the audience.

Your audience will be watching you as well as listening to you, of course, so use body language to your advantage. Natural, conversational gestures help you emphasize important ideas or direct the audience's attention to key visuals. Making eye contact with the audience is extremely important—doing so helps them feel a connection to you and your message, and it also helps you to monitor your audience's reaction. By making eye contact, you'll be able to tell whether the audience is paying close attention and whether they understand your message. Don't be afraid to move around as you speak—movement can help the audience stay focused on you— but avoid pacing back and forth or fidgeting, as these activities will distract them.

Dealing with Stage Fright

Another potential barrier to effective delivery is your level of anxiety about speaking in front of a group. Many people experience stage fright when asked to speak in front of a group, regardless of whether they are habitually nervous about communicating with others or they generally feel comfortable communicating.

Stage fright is most often a situational attack of anxiety that depends on factors such as

- the size of your audience;
- how well you know the people you are talking with;
- how well you know your subject;
- the status of the individuals you are talking with.

For example, you may feel relaxed when talking with a friend about a movie you saw the previous evening, but feel a sudden surge of panic when asked to describe your reaction to that same movie for a professor and your classmates in an English class. Or you may feel comfortable offering a lengthy response to a question from the professor during class, but feel extremely nervous about getting up in front of the class to give an oral presentation on that same topic.

To overcome nervousness before or during a presentation, try the following.

- *Develop a constructive attitude toward fear and anxiety.* Instead of wondering how you will get rid of these common emotions, ask yourself how you can use them. Individuals need tension—feelings of excitement and challenge—to increase their thinking ability and powers of concentration. Realize that everyone who speaks publicly experiences some apprehension and fear before speaking and that, in fact, some measure of anxiety is necessary for you to do your best. If you have ever participated in sports, this may sound familiar. Let the adrenaline energize your performance by using all that pent-up energy like fuel. Being nervous is similar to being excited, so channel your nervousness into a positive energy.

- *Grab every opportunity to practice and gain experience.* Whether you are snowboarding, building a Web site, or speaking in front of a group, knowledge of the requirements is likely to increase your comfort level. For example, you naturally will be more comfortable the tenth time you've gone scuba diving than the first time. Seek out opportunities to practice and gain experience. Sometimes this will be easier around people you know, but for some, it is easier to perform for an anonymous audience. Because you will be making your presentation in class, where you may know many but not all of your classmates, practice in both types of situations.

- *Prepare thoroughly for each presentation.* If you are worried about what you will say, how you will say it, *and* what the outcome will be, you certainly will be more anxious than if your *only* concern is about the outcome. Prepare. Rehearse. Be thorough. Then, when you rise to speak, you will be able to concentrate on the outcome. Control all the things you can control *before* the day of the presentation.

- *Concentrate on communicating with your audience.* Ask yourself, "How do I know that these individuals are hearing and understanding what I'm saying?" If, as you speak, you work hard to observe the reactions of your audience and to adapt to them, you will be much too busy to worry about your anxiety or fear.

- *Remember that your listeners want you to succeed.* Your listeners are just like you—friendly people. Just as they want to succeed when they get up to speak, they want you to do well when you speak. Even if you do make a slip, they will understand and forgive you! Not even the best speakers perform flawlessly every single time they speak. Do not hold yourself to an unreasonable standard, and remember that others are not holding you to that standard.

- *Keep in mind that it will be over more quickly than you expect.* You have prepared for days or weeks, but the presentation will be over in only a few minutes.

Polishing the Presentation

One of the best ways to alleviate nervousness and to be sure you are well prepared is to polish your presentation through rehearsal. It's best to have your presentation ready several days to a week in advance to allow time to practice several times in front of a mirror or your friends. Assuming that you intend to speak extemporaneously, use the first few rehearsals to test various phrasings of your ideas. As you start to feel comfortable with the flow of your presentation, begin to work on time. Most classroom assignments will give you a time limit or a range (say 3 to 5 minutes).

Develop your presentation with the middle of the range in mind. That is, if the range is 3 to 5 minutes, develop a presentation that requires 3 to 4 minutes to deliver during practice. When you make the actual presentation, you may find that because of audience reaction, impromptu remarks, and so on, the presentation takes longer than it did during rehearsal. You may also find, though, that you speak more quickly during the presentation than you did during practice. Pace yourself.

As the day of the actual presentation approaches, try to practice in the classroom where you will speak. This will add to your comfort level and allow you to anticipate the unexpected. This is especially important if you are using unfamiliar equipment, such as a microphone, presentation software, an overhead projector, or an LCD projector.

If you are extremely nervous or feel unsure about your ability to give a presentation, be proactive; address the problem early and directly. But keep in mind that you do have sources of support. Seek help from campus resources, such as the writing center or your instructor during office hours. Seek help well in advance of the due date. The night before the presentation is due is usually too late. Some of the advice in this chapter may not seem practical, but keep in mind that in most cases you will have at least a week, and often two or three, to complete an assignment. Don't forget that the instructor's goal is to help you learn and grow, and he or she understands that you may be nervous about presenting.

9 Presenting as a Group

Many of the oral presentations you give are culminations of group projects. Teachers often assign group work and expect an oral report as the end result. Group work is rewarding and emulates many job situations in which teams work on projects. But group work also presents challenges. Among these challenges are equally dividing the work, smoothly transitioning between multiple speakers, and adequately acknowledging nonspeaking (but contributing) group members.

Dividing the Work

Groups work best when members know and understand the roles they are expected to fill. Often instructors assign these roles, but just as often the group determines them. Even if the instructor does not assign specific tasks to various group members, the group should specify tasks for each member. This may be through nominating one member to act as a leader, who then assigns roles to each group member. Students may also volunteer to perform certain duties.

Having a leader is often useful because that person can coordinate communication among group members and with the instructor. A leader can also settle disputes or finalize decisions. The leader must strive to be objective and fair. Leading is a position not only of power but also of responsibility. The leader should gather contact information for all members of the group and set a schedule for achieving goals and deadlines. The leader need not dictate these goals, but should enforce any deadlines. Think of this person as a manager or film director.

The group should have one person serve as secretary or writer. The writer takes notes at all meetings (either as formal minutes or shorthand records). There may be a role for more than one writer in the group. One may serve as a secretary, while another compiles the group's research and composes that information in a draft. Another subset of the writer category could include production workers or designers. Designers build the visual aids and handouts the group will use during the presentation. They might also revise and proofread the final draft of the paper or check citation formats.

Both informative and persuasive group presentations require researchers. The researchers should spend time in the library, on the Web, and among peers or experts, taking notes and conducting interviews. The researchers should be responsible for gathering the raw materials used in the presentation. They should also be expected to double-check their information for reliability and credibility, and they should adequately cite their sources. If all members of the group are taking part in research, you may wish to divide the work; for example, two members of the group could conduct research at the library, while the other two members conduct an interview. The entire group could then gather to compare notes and decide on the best direction for the presentation.

When the time comes to give the presentation, one or more members of the group will need to speak. The instructor may require all members to speak during the presentation, but not always. Some group members may be more well versed in public speaking. Some may have more knowledge about specific areas of the presentation and be better suited to presenting that information orally. The speakers for the group should have the information they need well in advance of the presentation time. They should also be expected to have read the information several times and to have practiced speaking. If more than one person is speaking for the group, the speakers should also rehearse transitions between speakers.

Transitioning between Speakers

One mode of giving a group oral presentation is to have each speaking member talk in sequence. This very simple and straight-forward mode of delivery often works well. In this setup, however, group members should wrap up their section of the presentation with an introduction of the next member and offer some form of transition bridging the gap between the subtopics.

- ◆ "... and this is why I believe that living wills and Do Not Resuscitate orders should be respected by doctors, families, and the government. To offer another perspective, I now turn the floor over to Tricia. ..."

Another tactic is to have one group member serve as a sort of "master of ceremonies" or "emcee." The emcee introduces the topic of the discussion and then introduces each speaker in turn. One benefit of this arrangement is that the emcee can guide the pace of the presentation, urging rambling presenters to conclude or prompting terse presenters for more detail by asking questions or probing for more detail. The emcee can serve as a facilitator for a more interactive presentation as well. If the group decides to take questions during the presentation (rather than afterward), the emcee can field those questions and even direct them to the most qualified member of the group.

Groups should designate who will answer certain types of questions before they make their presentations. Some group members may be more qualified to field questions about research sources, while other group members may be better qualified to deal with on-the-spot application of the material to indirectly related material. Having a "go to" person for these types of questions helps avoid embarrassment and confusion during the presentation. Group members may freeze or come up blank due to stage fright or other pressures, so groups should devise a plan for dealing with these situations, including graceful and supportive methods for offering one another on-the-spot assistance.

These roles need not be exclusive. More than one group member can perform most of these roles. Likewise, any one group member can perform a number of roles within the group. A researcher may be a speaker, while the leader could also be a secretary.

Acknowledging Nonspeaking Group Members

Not every member of the group needs to speak during the presentation unless the instructor so requires. If certain members of the group do not speak during the presentation, the group leader or the emcee should mention the contributions of all members of the group. This can happen at the beginning or end of the presentation in a sort of summary. Alternatively, during the presentation the speakers may mention who performed what research or reference specific tasks and responsibilities. Whatever the case, it is good practice to know the names of your fellow group members. Transitions will be smoother if group members can refer to one another by name and do so occasionally throughout the presentation.

Nonspeaking members can help with other important tasks during the presentation, such as working the projector, passing out handouts, or demonstrating a process while one of the speakers explains.

10 *Evaluating Presentations*

In addition to your role as a presenter, you have another important role as an audience member for your classmates' presentations. You may be asked to evaluate their work, to offer suggestions for improvement, or even to demonstrate your understanding of the information they share. The following checklist will help you identify strengths and weaknesses in a presentation, both in the content and the speaker's delivery. As a student and a listener, you probably assess many of these strengths and weaknesses subconsciously. Being aware of the following components of a presentation (or paper) can change your mode of listening to one that is more active and critical.

At first, listening critically may seem like hard work, but as time goes on you will become comfortable and confident in this new style of listening. Paying attention to all of the items on this list is not easy or even advised. Instead, pay attention to the items that you already tend to notice and feel confident about evaluating. Pick a few other areas to concentrate on each time you hear a new speaker. Eventually, you will build better listening and analysis skills. A final recommendation: During a presentation, *make* (not *take*) notes. Writing every word the speaker says is never a good idea, but making comments in the margins of a handout or keeping a bulleted list or outline to trigger memories is very helpful, especially if you want to ask questions later.

Checklist for Evaluating a Presentation

The Speaker's Delivery

While the topic and the content are the most important parts of any presentation, the speaker has an incredible impact on the success of any presentation. The point is not to critique the speaker's every word or gesture; instead, note the places where the speaker's poise, demeanor, and performance help or hurt the presentation's message.

☐ **Voice**
  ☐ Can you understand the speaker?
  ☐ Is the speaker loud enough (but not too loud)?

☐ **Pace**
  ☐ Is the speaker's pace comfortable, not too fast or too slow?
  ☐ Does the speaker take time to allow for questions or repeat complex or confusing concepts?

☐ **Nervousness**
  ☐ Does the speaker seem relaxed and comfortable?
  ☐ Does the speaker avoid most meaningless filler words such as *uh* or *um*? (Do not nitpick, but is the number of *ums* distracting?)

☐ **Engagement with the audience**
  ☐ Does the speaker avoid simply reading his or her paper?
  ☐ Does the speaker make eye contact?
  ☐ Is the speaker aware of the audience's responses or reactions?
  ☐ Has the speaker adapted the material well for the audience?

☐ **Use of visual aids**
  ☐ Do the visual aids help you understand the speaker's message?

☐ Are the visual aids well designed and free of distracting or confusing elements?

☐ Does the speaker direct your attention to key points or visuals? Does the speaker adequately explain their significance?

Content and Coherence

Coherence refers to the degree to which all the parts and details in a paper or presentation work together toward the statement of purpose and thesis. If a presentation lacks coherence, it will seem to ramble all over and go off on tangents, not really making one clear point. A strong thesis and attention to coherence will make for a much stronger presentation.

☐ **Thesis**

    ☐ Is the thesis clearly expressed?

    ☐ Does the thesis make sense? Can you restate it in your own words?

    ☐ Is there only one apparent thesis or purpose?

    ☐ Do all of the main ideas go together?

☐ **Language choices**

    ☐ Does the speaker avoid using jargon?

    ☐ Does the speaker define key terms and unfamiliar words?

    ☐ Does the speaker address the audience using an appropriate and effective tone?

☐ **Transitions**

    ☐ Does the speaker clearly and smoothly link ideas and sections of the presentation?

    ☐ Are transitional words and phrases used correctly? For example, sometimes speakers overuse or misuse certain conjunctive adverbs in an attempt to sound more formal or "educated." The most common of these adverbs have very specific implications, as follows:

- *therefore* = because of what I just said
- *however* = in spite of what I just said
- *furthermore* = in addition to what I just said

☐ **Support**

    ☐ Does the speaker's support for his or her thesis make sense?

    ☐ Are examples and evidence appropriate and credible? Do they mean what the speaker says they mean?

    ☐ Do the examples and evidence support the speaker's claim(s)? Do you come to a similar conclusion based on these examples? Has the speaker mentioned other possible conclusions?

Argument and Persuasion

☐ **Does the speaker avoid logical fallacies? Does the speaker**

- offer only two options or solutions, when many more really may exist? (*false dilemma*)
- assume that an event that follows another event happens *because* of the first, even though this may not be true? (*post hoc ergo propter hoc,* "after this, therefore because of this")
- suggest that one decision will lead to more bad outcomes, even though there is very little evidence supporting this suggestion? For example, "if we legalize drugs, then everyone will have access to drugs all the time, and we will become a nation of drug addicts." (*slippery slope*)
- claim that something is true simply because most people believe that it is true? "Ninety-five percent of people surveyed believe that the sun does, in fact, revolve around the earth." (*popularity*)

- use other fallacies like these? (Books and Web sites about argument list many other fallacies. Consult your instructor if you have trouble understanding the occasionally complex definitions of some fallacies.)

☐ **Does the speaker seem credible and convincing?**

☐ **Do you agree with the speaker? Did the presentation make you change your opinion? Why or why not?**

☐ **Even if you disagree with the speaker, does the speaker adequately explain and defend his or her position?**

Thinking Critically about Your Own Presentation

The checklist above is a good guide for evaluating your own presentation too. One problem many people face when evaluating their own work is being too close to the material and too invested in the paper or the argument. A good way to evaluate your work critically is to distance yourself from it for a while. If possible, record yourself practicing the presentation, either on audio or video. Then spend a day or two (or longer if you have the time) not working on the project. When you return to the paper or presentation, read, view, or listen to the entire piece. Pretend that you are an audience member and use the above checklists to evaluate your own work. Do not be afraid to play devil's advocate and take an opposing view or to adopt a hostile attitude toward the presentation's message; however, rather than attacking all your own thoughts, ideas, and statements, instead be fair and tough. Envision how you would defend your ideas and statements to an audience member making the same kinds of critical comments and asking similarly probing questions. If you can, rework your project to anticipate and address these issues before making your presentation.